FOURTEEN GREATS

The Story of Jonah

A.J. Lykosh

MAKARIOS
PRESS

Esmont, VA

Makarios Press
P.O. Box 28, Esmont, VA 22937

© 2023 by A.J. Lykosh

All rights reserved. No part of this book may be reproduced in any form except in the case of brief quotations without written permission from Makarios Press.

Scripture in KJV unless otherwise stated.

Cover Illustration: Jonelle Lilly
Design: Nate Braxton

ISBN 978-1-956561-47-0

Printed in the United States of America

FOURTEEN GREATS

Great city.

Great wind.

Great tempest.

Great fear.

Great tempest.

Great fear.

Great fish.

Great city.

Great city.

Great ones.

Great ones.

Great evil.

Great joy.

Great city.

CONTENTS

Introduction 1
Prologue 3
Beginning 5
Flight 27
Return 89
Obedience 137
Response 185
Grace 217
After 259
Epilogue 263

CONTENTS

INTRODUCTION

The book of Jonah has no mysterious wheels within wheels, as in Ezekiel. No vivid dreams, as in Daniel. No extended poetic sermons, as in Jeremiah, Hosea, Nahum, and all the rest.
Unique among all the major and minor prophets, Jonah tells a story.
Just a story.
Four chapters—47 verses—tell the story of a man who hears clearly from God, but doesn't like what he hears and would prefer not to do what he's told, thank you very much.
He knows God, knows his word, knows his character—and yet runs from him.
Just a story—but what a story.
In the pages to come, we'll go through the entire book of Jonah, verse by verse.
I like free verse poetry, because the format allows either swift reading, or slow savoring.
One friend said, "I just read 40 pages in five minutes—and you know what? I'm okay with that!"

Another friend said, "I can't read your books quickly. It's like every page has a selah moment, a holy pause."

One friend lingers on a chapter, or even a specific poem, again and again, until she's ready to move on.

Another friend joyfully gets the tool he needs for his life, and goes out, better equipped.

No right or wrong way to read!

Directly below each poem's title, you'll find the specific verse out of Jonah that the poem refers to. Each of the 47 verses yielded at least one poem. Most yielded multiple.

Poems for specific words, for specific thoughts.

May you have as much blessing reading as I had preparing—how rich and beautiful is the God we serve.

— *AJ Lykosh*

PROLOGUE

As I was working on the first draft, full of enthusiasm for Jonah, I brought up the story with some new friends, enthusiastically talking about the scientific possibilities of the actual variety of whale, the comparative sizes of whale esophaguses, and the various stomachs of teethed whales compared to baleen whales.

Then the conversation shifted, and my friend had a specific take on Jonah.

"He prophesies a victory for Israel. He prophesies and it comes true. So he's famous in Israel as a prophet. He lives at a time of great civic national pride and patriotism, a time of, 'Go, Israel! We want victory! He's our prophet, and he predicted that God is on our side!'

"I think it's the same a lot today. A lot of churches have the same kind of patriotic national pride. The spirit of the air. And Jonah didn't want to go to Nineveh because he knew that God would use the Assyrians later against his own people. And then we have this book, ostensibly written by Jonah. Why do we have this book? Because he survived the fish, and the trip to

Nineveh and the plant, and he ended up back in Israel to write the scroll with this question, very humbled. I think he learned the lesson and began to worship God, and then showed how ridiculous his civic national pride had been."

As I listened to him, I started to get agitated inside.

Because his statement wasn't bad. If anything, it was far more sophisticated than the superficial, "Look at horrible Jonah—what a rebellious heart he carried" perspective that I find more often.

And yet, though I didn't have words at the time for why his perspective frustrated me ... it did frustrate me.

More on that to come.

For now ... the story itself.

BEGINNING

Becoming

Now the word of the LORD came unto Jonah the son of Amittai, saying,

The first word in Hebrew:
Haya.

Becoming.
Established.

Come into being.
Come to pass.

The word of the LORD didn't just "arrive,"
But it came with the power and authority to establish.

The same word in Genesis 1:3,
"Let there *be* light."

A birthday greeting comes.
By contrast, an eviction notice also comes ...

But it comes with teeth
And authority to accomplish.

The Word for "Word"

*Now the word of the LORD came unto Jonah the
    son of Amittai, saying,*

The word for "word" is common in the
    Hebrew, used for God and man,
From the tower of Babel in Genesis at
    the beginning
To the scolding prophet Malachi at the end,
A total of 1,455 times.

Wearisome words by a rebellious people,
Strong words by the mouths of the
    prophets ...

But the word of the LORD is
    something else.

The Word of the LORD

*Now the word of the LORD came unto Jonah the
son of Amittai, saying,*

The specific phrase "the word of the LORD"
    occurs 145 times in the Old Testament,
An exact ten percent of the uses of "word,"
In 26 of the 39 books,[1]
Beginning with Abraham:
"After these things
The word of the LORD
Came unto Abram in a vision, saying,
Fear not, Abram:
I *am* thy shield,
And thy exceeding great reward."[2]

The last Old Testament book of
    Malachi opens:
"The burden of the word of the LORD to
    Israel by Malachi."[3]

The Tetragrammaton

Now the word of the LORD came unto Jonah the son of Amittai, saying,

The LORD.
Yahweh.
Four Hebrew letters:
Yod-Hei-Vav-Hei.

Each letter in Hebrew means something.
Yod for *hand.*
Vav for *connector, hook,* or *spike.*
Hei for *behold.*

Hand, behold, connector, behold.
The four-letter Tetragrammaton:
Each of the 6,521 uses
Points to the coming Messiah:

Behold the hand.
Behold the spike.

The Prophet's Name and Genealogy

Now the word of the LORD came unto Jonah the son of Amittai, saying,

Jonah's name meant *dove*.
A term of endearment, a bird of gentleness.

Ah, well.

His story was full of mischievous reversals.
Might as well start with his name.

Note another Old Testament dove:
The bird Noah sent out from the ark to see
 if the waters had abated.

Another watery dove connection.

Jonah, son of Amittai, whose name
 meant *my truth*.
Son of a truth-teller.

Jonah, too, spoke the truth,
Though he spoke truth so clearly

without love,

We're left almost breathless.

A Quick History Lesson

Now the word of the LORD came unto Jonah the son of Amittai, saying,

After the kings Saul, David, and Solomon, Solomon's son Rehoboam spoke harshly to his people.

Judah and Benjamin stayed with him and formed Judah;
The other ten tribes left to form Israel.

The names can be tricky.
Long before, the third Patriarch, Jacob, was renamed Israel.
His twelve children made up the twelve tribes of Israel.
The Israelites left Egypt under Moses,
Then conquered the promised land under Joshua.
Later, when they divided, only part of the Israelites were then "Israel."

Judah's capital was Jerusalem.
Israel's capital was Samaria.

The leader of newly formed Israel, Jeroboam,
Immediately established idol worship,
So the priests and Levites
And those faithful to the God of
    their ancestors
Fled to Judah.

In the generations that followed,
Judah occasionally had a king that
    looked to God.
Israel never did.

Jonah lived in Israel, and prophesied to King
    Jeroboam II in Samaria.
This Jeroboam, predictably, did evil in the
    eyes of the Lord.

The Record of the Scripture

*Now the word of the LORD came unto Jonah the
son of Amittai, saying,*

The scriptural record about the geopolitical
    situation:
"Jeroboam son of Jehoash king of Israel
    became king in Samaria,
And he reigned forty-one years.
He did evil in the eyes of the Lord
And did not turn away from any of the sins
    of Jeroboam son of Nebat,
Which he had caused Israel to commit.
He was the one who restored the boundaries
    of Israel
From Lebo Hamath to the Dead Sea,
In accordance with the word of the Lord,
    the God of Israel,
Spoken through his servant Jonah son
    of Amittai,
The prophet from Gath Hepher.

The Lord had seen how bitterly everyone
    in Israel,
Whether slave or free, was suffering;
There was no one to help them.

And since the Lord had
Not said
He would blot out the name of Israel from
   under heaven,
He saved them by the hand of Jeroboam son
   of Jehoash.

As for the other events of Jeroboam's reign,
   all he did,
And his military achievements,
Including how he recovered for Israel both
   Damascus and Hamath,
Which had belonged to Judah,
Are they not written in the book of the
   annals of the kings of Israel?
Jeroboam rested with his ancestors, the
   kings of Israel.
And Zechariah his son succeeded him
   as king."[4]

Piecing Together Clues

*Now the word of the LORD came unto Jonah the
son of Amittai, saying,*

Jeroboam II ruled thirteen years longer than
any other king of Israel.
The runner-up, Jehu, ruled 28 years.
Long rule isn't necessarily a sign of favor:
The evil king Manasseh ruled the southern
kingdom of Judah for 55 years.

The scripture does not detail the story of
military success,
But in outline form:

Jonah prophesied that Jeroboam II would
have success
Restoring the boundaries.

Years before, Solomon, bordered on the west
by the Mediterranean,
Controlled all the lands
From the Euphrates in the east,
To the land of the Philistines—Lebanon and
Syria—in the north,
To Egypt in the south.[5]

But when Solomon started to worship
  other gods,
His kingdom started to erode.
He lost Damascus to the rebel Rezon
  of Zobah.[6]

Now, over 150 years later, Jeroboam II took
  Damascus back.[7]

Jonah's prophecy came true.

But the real hero of this story is Yahweh.
"The Lord had seen how bitterly everyone
  in Israel,
Whether slave or free, was suffering;
There was no one to help them."[8]

He sent encouragement to the king through
  the mouth of Jonah.

And since God hadn't said he'd wipe
  out Israel,
He saved them …

Using the unrighteous hand of Jeroboam II.

God works his purposes,
Using all sorts of unexpected means.

The Prophet's Hometown

*Now the word of the LORD came unto Jonah the
son of Amittai, saying,*

Jonah came from Gath Hepher,[9]
Three miles from Nazareth,
In the region of Galilee.

Many years later, grumpy Pharisees
Asked Nicodemus, a secret Jesus-follower,
"Look into it,
And you will find that a prophet does not
    come out of Galilee."[10]

Oops.

Jonah came from Galilee.

So did Hosea.

Also, perhaps, Elijah, Elisha, and Amos.[11]

Galilee: not only a fertile land for
    prophetic words,
But also pre-figuring another
    prophet to come.

The Typical Expectation

Now the word of the LORD came unto Jonah the son of Amittai, saying,

In sixteen of the seventeen prophetic books,
Major Prophets
(Isaiah, Jeremiah and his book of
    Lamentations, Ezekiel, Daniel)
And Minor Prophets
(Hosea, Joel, Amos, Obadiah, Micah,
    Nahum, Habakkuk, Zephaniah, Haggai,
    Zechariah, Malachi),
The word of the Lord forms the bulk
    of the book.

Hear the word of the Lord in the mouth of
    his prophets.

Not here.

Unique among the prophets,
Jonah tells the story of the prophet.

Narrative,
Not prophetic declaration.

The Message

Arise, go to Nineveh, that great city, and cry against it; for their wickedness is come up before me.

The Hebrew begins with these two verbs:

Arise!
Go!

Rise up, stand up, get up!
Go! Walk!

To Nineveh, that great city,
A city proud, large, important, haughty, insolent.[12]

And cry, call, proclaim against it.

Don't whisper the coming judgment,
But yell it out!
Shout a proclamation!

Her evil, wickedness, mischief
Has come up before me.

The First Great

Arise, go to Nineveh, that great city, and cry against it; for their wickedness is come up before me.

The number one signifies Commencement.

The first of the fourteen uses of Great:

That great city.
Significant.

Driving the action.

Faces

Arise, go to Nineveh, that great city, and cry against it; for their wickedness is come up before me.

In the Hebrew,
The evil of the city ascends
"To my faces."

Rabbi Lapin pointed out
That Hebrew has no singular word
"Face."[13]

The word is always plural, "faces,"
A constant reminder
That no one has only one face.

Our faces change constantly:
Not only from birth to old age,
But also from interaction and emotion.

Even God has faces,
And though here he proclaims judgment,
What other faces might he yet reveal?

About Nineveh

Arise, go to Nineveh, that great city, and cry against it; for their wickedness is come up before me.

Centuries earlier, Noah exited the ark,
With his sons Shem, Ham, and Japheth.

Ham fathered Cush.
Cush fathered Nimrod.

Nimrod founded Babylon
And, later, Nineveh, in the land of Assyria.[14]

Geographically situated on the east bank of
  the Tigris River,
Encircled by the modern city of
  Mosul, in Iraq.[15]

At the time of Jonah, centuries
  after Nimrod,
The specter of the Assyrians had
  started to loom,

Culminating, about eighty years after Jonah,
With the fall of Israel.

Though the scriptures stay silent about
   specific atrocities,
The Assyrians themselves wrote about
   their warfare.
"A pyramid of heads I reared in front
   of the city.
Their youths and their maidens I burnt up
   in the flames."

"I flayed [a king I defeated],
His skin I spread upon the wall of
   the city."[16]

Practices so ugly, so inhuman,
Even reading about them turns the stomach.

Who would want to be their neighbor?

Not an Easy Call

Arise, go to Nineveh, that great city, and cry against it; for their wickedness is come up before me.

Imagine:

In 1951: Go to Moscow and preach against the Soviets.
In 1971: Go to Beijing and preach against the Chinese Communist Party.
In 1976: Go to Phnom Penh and preach against the Khmer Rouge.
In 1996: Go to Kandahar and preach against the Taliban.
In 2011: Go to Nigeria and preach against Boko Haram.

Go to the most violent, most cruel, most genocide-minded people,
And tell them that they're wrong.

Not an easy call.

FLIGHT

Opposite

But Jonah rose up to flee unto Tarshish from the presence of the LORD, and went down to Joppa; and he found a ship going to Tarshish: so he paid the fare thereof, and went down into it, to go with them unto Tarshish from the presence of the LORD.

In the Hebrew, the connection is clear.

The LORD said: Arise, go to Nineveh.
Qum yalak el Nineveh.

Jonah did
Arise.

But he fled.
Qum barah Tarshish.

He was supposed to go east across the land
   of the Middle East peninsula,
From the Mediterranean coast to Iraq.

Rather, he went west across the water of the
   Mediterranean Sea,
From the Mediterranean coast, going to the

farthest known western point.[17]

As opposite as he could go.

Travel Plans

But Jonah rose up to flee unto Tarshish from the presence of the LORD, and went down to Joppa; and he found a ship going to Tarshish: so he paid the fare thereof, and went down into it, to go with them unto Tarshish from the presence of the LORD.

First to the Israeli port city of Jaffa,
The port-of-entry for the cedars of Lebanon,
Both for Solomon's Temple,
And the second Temple of Jerusalem.[18]

No majestic tree of strength here—
The man of God was fleeing.

The Ship

> But Jonah rose up to flee unto Tarshish from
> the presence of the LORD, and went down to
> Joppa; and he found a ship going to Tarshish:
> so he paid the fare thereof, and went down
> into it, to go with them unto Tarshish from the
> presence of the LORD.

In ancient times, many ships stayed in sight
of the shore.
With primitive navigation, travel along the
coast made sense.

But the Tarshish ships were known as large,
ocean-going ships,
Ready to trade.

Picture: Jonah fled headlong and in haste,
Eager to get as far away as possible.

No coast-hugger;
He wanted the open sea.

Descent

*But Jonah rose up to flee unto Tarshish from
the presence of the LORD, and went down to
Joppa; and he found a ship going to Tarshish:
so he paid the fare thereof, and went down
into it, to go with them unto Tarshish from the
presence of the LORD.*

In the Hebrew, the connection is clear:
The LORD said to arise, to rise up.

But twice in the next verse, Jonah
Descended.

First he went down to Joppa.
Then he went down into the ship.

So clever of the author,
The rhetorical flourish to emphasize
 opposites.

Up,
Down.

Obedient,
Naughty.

Pointedly Foolish

But Jonah rose up to flee unto Tarshish from the presence of the LORD, and went down to Joppa; and he found a ship going to Tarshish: so he paid the fare thereof, and went down into it, to go with them unto Tarshish from the presence of the LORD.

In the Hebrew, the connection is clear:

The Ninevite evil ascended
To the faces of Yahweh.

One verse later, Jonah ran away
From the faces of Yahweh.

And just in case the first mention
    wasn't enough,
The author says this twice.

Running away toward Tarshish from the
    faces of Yahweh.
Going toward Tarshish from the faces
    of Yahweh.

Did Jonah really think this would work?

That the Ninevite evil might ascend,

But not his own personal rebellion?

Motivation

But Jonah rose up to flee unto Tarshish from the presence of the LORD, and went down to Joppa; and he found a ship going to Tarshish: so he paid the fare thereof, and went down into it, to go with them unto Tarshish from the presence of the LORD.

Why flee from the presence of the LORD?
Why do something so pointedly foolish?

Jonah was an Old Testament prophet.
He could see the future.

He knew God,
And believed what God said about his character.

"Assyria was to be God's sword of judgment against Israel.
If Nineveh perished, Israel might be saved.
God's mercy might arrest this overthrow of Nineveh.
Was this why Jonah would sacrifice himself to save his nation?"[19]

Had he counted the cost,
Now giving his life to save his people,
Even paying the fare, because that was a
    small price to pay?

Perhaps.

Or perhaps he simply disliked how the
    Assyrians treated others,
And had a strong bent for justice.

Remember the commentary about the rule
    of Jeroboam II:
"The Lord had seen how bitterly everyone
    in Israel,
Whether slave or free, was suffering;
There was no one to help them."[20]

The Israelites were oppressed on all sides,
And undoubtedly reports of Assyrian
    atrocities reached him.

In any case ... he fled.

The Second and Third Greats

> But the LORD sent out a great wind into the sea, and there was a mighty tempest in the sea, so that the ship was like to be broken.

In the Hebrew, the connection is clear:

Jonah was supposed to go to a great city.
Instead he met with a great wind and a
  great tempest,

A wind and a tempest
Large in magnitude and extent,
  intense, loud.[21]

In the Hebrew, at the beginning,
The word of the LORD was "becoming."

Now the mighty tempest is "becoming."
Jonah fled, so the LORD cast down a
  great wind.

Wind

*But the LORD sent out a great wind into the
sea, and there was a mighty tempest in the sea,
so that the ship was like to be broken.*

The LORD sent a great wind,
A great *ruach*.

The word often translated "Spirit,"
The third member of the Godhead.

An invisible force,
Manifesting in various ways,

Unseen but in the results,
"Invisible except by its manifestations."[22]

Destroy

But the LORD sent out a great wind into the sea, and there was a mighty tempest in the sea, so that the ship was like to be broken.

Centuries later, Jesus taught,
"The thief comes only to steal and kill
 and destroy;
I have come that they may have life, and
 have it to the full."[23]

Yet here the LORD sent a storm to
 oppose Jonah,
So that the ship was about to be broken in
 pieces, destroyed.

Notice the challenge to discernment:
The thief comes to destroy, with the end
 result destruction.
The LORD sometimes sends a storm, with
 the end result:

Restoration.

Old Salts

*Then the mariners were afraid, and cried every
man unto his god, and cast forth the wares
that were in the ship into the sea, to lighten
it of them. But Jonah was gone down into
the sides of the ship; and he lay, and was
fast asleep.*

Charmingly, the Hebrew word for "mariner"
Comes from the word "salt."

The Mediterranean Sea, because of high
  evaporation
And low influx of freshwater,
Has high salinity.[24]

Sailors in the Mediterranean sail the salt sea.

But besides the literal, Jesus taught:
"You are the salt of the earth.
But if the salt loses its saltiness,
How can it be made salty again?
It is no longer good for anything,
Except to be thrown out and trampled
  underfoot."[25]

The sailors worshipped as best they could,

But the only one who carried the truth
Had, apparently, lost his saltiness.

Reverent Awe

Then the mariners were afraid, and cried every man unto his god, and cast forth the wares that were in the ship into the sea, to lighten it of them. But Jonah was gone down into the sides of the ship; and he lay, and was fast asleep.

The sailors stood in awe of the storm,
Fearful, afraid, terrified,
In astonishment and reverence.

The same fear Adam felt, after eating
   the fruit:
"I was afraid, because I was naked; and I
   hid myself."[26]

The same fear Sarah felt, after she laughed at
   the prophetic word
That she would have a son in her old age.[27]

The sailors recognized the severity of
   the storm,
And acted out of reverent awe,
Calling on their gods, pleading for change.

Not the same cry of proclamation God
 gave to Jonah,
But a cry for help.

A Cry for Help

Then the mariners were afraid, and cried every man unto his god, and cast forth the wares that were in the ship into the sea, to lighten it of them. But Jonah was gone down into the sides of the ship; and he lay, and was fast asleep.

The mariners "cried" for help.

Centuries earlier, Moses wrote of another people in distress:

"And it came to pass in process of time,
That the king of Egypt died:
And the children of Israel sighed by reason of the bondage,
And they cried,
And their cry came up unto God by reason of the bondage.
And God heard their groaning,
And God remembered his covenant
With Abraham,
With Isaac, and
With Jacob."[28]

God heard the cry for help out of Egypt.
He remembered his covenant with the
 Patriarchs.
But would he hear the cry for help out of the
 Mediterranean?
With a group of people who have
 no covenant?
Indeed, don't even know his name?

Just what cries for help does God hear?

No Blessing

*Then the mariners were afraid, and cried every
man unto his god, and cast forth the wares
that were in the ship into the sea, to lighten
it of them. But Jonah was gone down into
the sides of the ship; and he lay, and was
fast asleep.*

The LORD had cast forth the great wind,
And in response, the sailors cast forth their
   trading goods.

They sacrificed the entire reason for
   their voyage,
Getting rid of all potential profit in hope to
   spare their lives.

God had promised Abraham:
"I will bless those who bless you,
And whoever curses you I will curse;
And all peoples on earth
Will be blessed through you."[29]

Here a descendent of Abraham
Was not blessing the peoples on earth.
His presence was, rather, a curse on them.

Oblivious

Then the mariners were afraid, and cried every man unto his god, and cast forth the wares that were in the ship into the sea, to lighten it of them. But Jonah was gone down into the sides of the ship; and he lay, and was fast asleep.

Once again, the reminder:
Jonah had
Gone down
Into the recesses of the ship,
Where he lay
Asleep.

This was not a normal nap.

Of the nine biblical Hebrew words for sleep,
This word means "stupefied, as in sleep
  or death."
Unconscious, heavy sleep.

Sisera, fleeing from the army of Barak,
Fell into this stupefaction,
And Jael killed him.[30]

Daniel twice described himself thus,
While in a prophetic trance.[31]

While the sailors had done
All they could
To save themselves from the storm,

Jonah was passed out belowdecks,
Entirely unaware of the storm's existence.

Again, Arise

So the shipmaster came to him, and said unto him, What meanest thou, O sleeper? arise, call upon thy God, if so be that God will think upon us, that we perish not.

The captain of the ship came to Jonah and
 first gave a little reprimand:
"What are you doing, stupefied one?"

Then he repeated two exact commands of
 the word of the LORD:
Arise.
Cry.

But do not cry to the people of Nineveh.
Cry to your God.

Perhaps, peradventure,
God will think on us, shine on us,
That we perish not.

Who knows? Maybe your God
Will be the one to save.

An Appropriate Appellation

So the shipmaster came to him, and said unto him, What meanest thou, O sleeper? arise, call upon thy God, if so be that God will think upon us, that we perish not.

In some translations, the captain asked:
"How can you sleep?"[32]
"How is it that you are sleeping?"[33]

In some translations, the captain called
 Jonah out by his action:
"What do you mean, you sleeper?"[34]
"What are you [doing], O sleeper?"[35]

What a name to be called:
The befuddled one,
The unconscious,
The sleeper.

Your mind must be turned off,
To think any flight of yours could work.

Evil

And they said every one to his fellow, Come, and let us cast lots, that we may know for whose cause this evil is upon us. So they cast lots, and the lot fell upon Jonah.

Who brought this evil upon us?

This word "evil":
Wicked, injurious,
"Breaking up all that is good or desirable; Injurious to all others."[36]
Calamity.

Interesting to note that the Lord brought
This evil.

Not capriciously.
Purposefully.

Cast Lots

And they said every one to his fellow, Come, and let us cast lots, that we may know for whose cause this evil is upon us. So they cast lots, and the lot fell upon Jonah.

To cast lots,
Toss a pebble.

Useful
To divide garments,
To determine the guilty,
To decide the land allotment,
To deduce the auspicious day.

Flip a quarter, and go from there!

No longer a typical way to seek
Greater revelation:

And yet ...

"The lot is cast into the lap,
But its every decision is from the LORD."[37]

"We may throw the dice,
But the LORD determines how they fall."[38]

We've Tried Everything Else

*And they said every one to his fellow, Come, and
let us cast lots, that we may know for whose
cause this evil is upon us. So they cast lots,
and the lot fell upon Jonah.*

Once the sailors had done all they could do,
They assumed the storm had
    supernatural origins,
And sought to determine the cause.

Inherent in the action:
The assumption that every action had
    an origin.
If there was an evil, there was a cause
    of the evil.

While the law of sowing and reaping is a
    general truth,
Of course not every seed sprouts.

This idea that every evil had a cause:
No grace here.

The baby died
Because the parents sinned.

Or if the young mother died,
Seek the curse, from herself, or her family
   line, or an enemy.

The story of Jonah does not overturn
This uncomfortable assumption.

The Full Counsel of God

And they said every one to his fellow, Come, and let us cast lots, that we may know for whose cause this evil is upon us. So they cast lots, and the lot fell upon Jonah.

Though the book of Jonah does not overturn
The incorrect doctrine of
Assumed cause and effect,

Don't take this one story as
The sum total of how the world works.

The book of Job, for example, does overturn
    this doctrine.
The righteous man, brought to harm,
Sought to defend himself from his friends,
Who kept trying to persuade him
That his calamities were all his fault.

Wrong.

In Job, we find the background of a cosmic
    challenge,
The accuser told God that Job loved God
Only because God did good things for him.

Job came to harm *because* of his
righteousness.

The life of Jesus, too, overturns
this doctrine.
We find Jesus, after a time of ministry,
Sought to cross the Sea of Galilee,
When, as in Jonah, a storm kicked up.
"He got up, rebuked the wind and said to
the waves, 'Quiet! Be still!'
Then the wind died down and it was
completely calm."[39]

The "rebuke" was the same word used
When Jesus drove out demons.
A demonically inspired retributive storm.

Not because Jesus deserved it,
But because an enemy opposes.

Not to mention that righteous Jesus
Suffered for the sins of the whole world—
Not for his actions, but for ours.

Sometimes there is an effect
Without a cause.

But sometimes there is a cause and effect.

God speaks in the book of Isaiah:
"I form the light and create darkness,
I bring prosperity and create disaster;

I, the LORD, do all these things."[40]

Sometimes the disasters are from
  the LORD ...
As in the book of Jonah.

Work

Then said they unto him, Tell us, we pray thee, for whose cause this evil is upon us; What is thine occupation? and whence comest thou? what is thy country? and of what people art thou?

What is Jonah's work?

The first time scripture used that word for work, we find:
"And on the seventh day God ended his work which he had made;
And he rested on the seventh day from all his work which he had made." [41]

God's work is creating and sustaining,
Work and rest, in perfect alignment.

What is Jonah's work?

Not what he's doing now.
Completely out of alignment.

Questions

Then said they unto him, Tell us, we pray thee, for whose cause this evil is upon us; What is thine occupation? and whence comest thou? what is thy country? and of what people art thou?

"Please, we entreat you, tell us why this trip has come to disaster.
What is your work?
Where did you come from?
What is your land?
Who are your people?"

Answers

And he said unto them, I am an Hebrew; and I fear the LORD, the God of heaven, which hath made the sea and the dry land.

Jonah answered only the last question:
"Who are your people?"

I am a Hebrew, a descendant of Abraham.

He sidestepped three questions:
"What is your work?
Where did you come from?
What is your land?"

Instead, he answered the necessary,
  unasked question:
"Who is your God?"

The God of Heaven

And he said unto them, I am an Hebrew; and I fear the LORD, the God of heaven, which hath made the sea and the dry land.

When Jonah said, "I fear the LORD, the
  God of heaven,"
The title seems obvious to us.

But scripture only uses this title
  twenty-one times,
All of them during the time of the Gentiles,
"When God acted from heaven,
Not from the mercy seat in the tabernacle
  or temple."[42]

Meaning: for a long time,
God lived among his people and was
  their God.
Now, though, he had withdrawn to heaven.

In Jonah's mouth, it sounded like a title, not
  of majesty,
But of disappointment and bitterness.

"I fear the LORD, the God far away,
Who made the sea and the dry land."

Fear

And he said unto them, I am an Hebrew; and I fear the LORD, the God of heaven, which hath made the sea and the dry land.

The mariners feared the tempest.
Jonah used the same word to say that he had
 fears, too.

The mariners had external evidence of
 their fear:
They sought to work and worship.

Jonah had no external evidence of his fear.
He had slept deeply.

But in fairness to him,
Perhaps he fell into his deep sleep

Because of the inner dread of trying to
 escape the inescapable,
The wish for a way out—

Even knowing that no way out existed.

Whom Shall I Fear

And he said unto them, I am an Hebrew; and I fear the LORD, the God of heaven, which hath made the sea and the dry land.

Jonah feared Yahweh,
The Self-Existing One,
The Eternal.

He is the God, the Ruler, the Judge
Of heaven, the lofty place,
Both visible sky and the place God dwells.

He made, produced, fashioned
The sea, which he gathered together,
And the dry land.[43]

The Men

Then were the men exceedingly afraid, and said unto him. Why hast thou done this? For the men knew that he fled from the presence of the LORD, because he had told them.

The Hebrew scripture uses four words
for "man."

One, *Adam*, refers to his origin: coming
from the dust of the *Adamah*, the ground.
One, *Ish*, refers to his gender: male.
One, *Geber*, refers to his strength: mighty.
And the last, the one used here.

Enosh, infirmities, both physical and moral.
Man both mortal and incurably corrupt in
character.

The text could have said that
These were men of clay.

Rather, it draws attention to the fact that
these were
Morally depraved and physically
faltering men.

And yet they consistently act in contradiction to this description.

One commentary described the book of Jonah as satire,[44]
Which uses "humor, irony, exaggeration, or ridicule
To expose and criticize people's stupidity or vices."[45]

Definite irony here:
The morally corrupt men were trying to walk with God.

The Fourth Great

Then were the men exceedingly afraid, and said unto him. Why hast thou done this? For the men knew that he fled from the presence of the LORD, because he had told them.

From the great city,
To great wind and great tempest,
Now the sailors showed great fear.

In the Hebrew:
"And they are fearing, the mortals fear great."[46]
"They feared a great fear."

The same word for "fear," doubled for emphasis.

They already feared, but
Now their fear increased.

The Faces of Yahweh

Then were the men exceedingly afraid, and said unto him. Why hast thou done this? For the men knew that he fled from the presence of the LORD, because he had told them.

The men knew that Jonah fled from the
    faces of Yahweh,
"Because he had told them."

When did he tell them?

Two possible answers.

One possibility:
He may have told them now,
After he reported that he served
"The LORD, the God of heaven,"
And mentioned that he had been fleeing
    from God's faces.

The other possibility:

He may have told them earlier.

"Why are you heading to Tarshish?"

"God asked me to do something that I didn't want to do."

"Oh! We don't hear that answer very often."

Whenever Jonah happened to share this bit
   of backstory,
The mariners now came face-to-face with
   the reality
That his God was real, and powerful, and Corrective.

Why

Then were the men exceedingly afraid, and said unto him. Why hast thou done this? For the men knew that he fled from the presence of the LORD, because he had told them.

The mariners gave an interesting reply.

The first word could be both interrogative, questioning.
"Why?"
Like, "What reason did you have to flee? Do tell!"
An invitation to conversation.

Alternately, that first word could be exclamation, sudden utterance.
"WHY!"
Like, "What were you thinking?"
Which required no response.

What He Made

Then were the men exceedingly afraid, and said unto him. Why hast thou done this? For the men knew that he fled from the presence of the LORD, because he had told them.

In the previous verse,
Jonah said that God "made the sea and the dry land."

Here the mariners use the same word:
"Why have you made this?"

God made the sea and dry land,
And you made this storm.

No Answer

Then were the men exceedingly afraid, and said unto him. Why hast thou done this? For the men knew that he fled from the presence of the LORD, because he had told them.

Jonah gave no recorded answer.
Nothing to say.

Next Question

Then said they unto him, What shall we do unto thee, that the sea may be calm unto us? for the sea wrought, and was tempestuous.

Your God made the world.
Your actions made this storm.
What shall we make?

Same word.
Three active entities:
God, Jonah, the mariners.

There Is Always a Solution

Then said they unto him, What shall we do unto thee, that the sea may be calm unto us? for the sea wrought, and was tempestuous.

How unexpected, in the face of such
   a tempest,
To find that the mariners had no doubt
That a solution existed.

Their logical conclusion:
If Jonah's action caused the sea to rage,
Surely there must be a solution to settle it.

Kindness?

And he said unto them, Take me up, and cast me forth into the sea; so shall the sea be calm unto you: for I know that for my sake this great tempest is upon you.

How to settle a storm?

"Toss me overboard.
God, apparently, wants a sacrifice,
And as the instigator,
I'm the issue."

A noble action?
Perhaps.

Or maybe resigned:
It was a long shot to begin with,
Thinking I could outrun God.

Or does Jonah celebrate a secret
 triumph here?
Whatever happens next,
At least I'm not heading to Nineveh!

The Fifth Great

And he said unto them, Take me up, and cast me forth into the sea; so shall the sea be calm unto you: for I know that for my sake this great tempest is upon you.

The number five:

Divine grace.

Great tempest as divine grace?

Not to all appearances...

But this story is not done yet.

A Lot of Knowing

And he said unto them, Take me up, and cast me forth into the sea; so shall the sea be calm unto you: for I know that for my sake this great tempest is upon you.

First the mariners cast lots to know the storm's cause.

They knew that Jonah fled from the presence of the LORD.

Then Jonah knew that the tempest was on his account.

They all came to certainty.

Best Effort

*Nevertheless the men rowed hard to bring it
to the land; but they could not: for the sea
wrought, and was tempestuous against them.*

Initially rejecting the easy course of action,
The mariners rowed hard,
Seeking the dry land that the
    LORD created.

Presumably, by this time, any masts and sails
    were gone.

In the days of Moses,
God made a path through the sea ...
But in the days of Jonah, this was not to be.

By Contrast

Wherefore they cried unto the LORD, and said,
We beseech thee, O LORD, we beseech thee,
let us not perish for this man's life, and lay not
upon us innocent blood: for thou, O LORD,
hast done as it pleased thee.

The mariner's cried to Yahweh.
No record of what Jonah did.

No rowing.
No prayers of any kind.

For all we know,
Jonah remained silent and still.

We Beseech You

*Wherefore they cried unto the LORD, and said,
We beseech thee, O LORD, we beseech thee,
let us not perish for this man's life, and lay not
upon us innocent blood: for thou, O LORD,
hast done as it pleased thee.*

Twice the mariners fervently asked Yahweh
That they not be destroyed for Jonah's life.
"If he is guilty, don't let us die, too!"

They recognized the possibility that they
    misunderstood:
He might be innocent.
"If he is innocent, don't destroy us on
    his behalf.

Yahweh, you have made what you desired.
We are seeking to respond in the best
    possible way
With incomplete information."

Like almost every person
In every time
And every place.

Obedient

So they took up Jonah, and cast him forth into the sea: and the sea ceased from her raging.

The sailors did exactly as Jonah said:
They took him up and cast him forth.
Same words in the Hebrew.
Precisely obedient.

Why?

So they took up Jonah, and cast him forth into the sea: and the sea ceased from her raging.

Why, if Jonah knew he was the problem,
Did he not simply jump over on his own?

Several possibilities.

Uncertainty.
Though it's easy enough to tell a story with
Logical cause and effect,
In the midst of the day-to-day,
Events are more murky.
Was this *really* caused by God?
Or simply an unfortunate chance?
But Jonah heard from God clearly,
So perhaps he struggled less with
   uncertainty.

Sin.
"You shall not murder."[47]
What is unlawful for you to do for another
Is also unlawful for you to do for yourself.
Thus, suicide is murder.
Murder is different than going down with

all hands on deck ...
Even though the latter involved more lives.
Atonement.
The sailors wanted to rid themselves of
   their guilt.
To do that, they needed an effective
   sacrifice,
And Jonah had offered himself.
Lacking other choices,
They made the necessary sacrifice.

Between the Lines

So they took up Jonah, and cast him forth into the sea: and the sea ceased from her raging.

In my childhood, I assumed that Jonah lived.
I thought that being tossed overboard was
   sufficient to appease
Offended deity.

I imagined a thorough wetting,
Then a wave to the sailors on deck as he
   started swimming toward shore
Through peaceful waters ... and soon to
   receive help in the form of a passing whale.

No. This was the fanciful picture of a
   Disney movie,[48]
Not the obvious, albeit unstated, fact:
Jonah, as the sacrifice,

Died

Between the first half of the sentence
And the second.

Rage

*So they took up Jonah, and cast him forth into
the sea: and the sea ceased from her raging.*

Make the sacrifice, and

The sea's rage ended.
The sea's indignation stopped.
The sea's wrath ceased.

Ceased

So they took up Jonah, and cast him forth into the sea: and the sea ceased from her raging.

The Hebrew word for "cease"
Means "stop."

As in:
Stand still, stop moving, stand firm.

A normal storm gradually tapers off.
All the stored-up kinetic energy gradually
  dissipates,
As the tall waves become small waves,
And eventually calm returns.

This description seems more epic:
The raging sea stood still.

The Sixth Great

*Then the men feared the LORD exceedingly,
and offered a sacrifice unto the LORD, and
made vows.*

Again, in the Hebrew:
"And they are fearing, the mortals
 fear great."[49]
"They feared a great fear."

First they feared this great fear when they
 heard of the true God.
Now they saw with their own eyes,
And they feared a great fear.

And their response, in the Hebrew:
"They sacrificed a sacrifice,
And vowed a vow."

The natural human response
To the power of the God,
In this sixth great, the number of man.

Foreshadowing

*Then the men feared the LORD exceedingly,
and offered a sacrifice unto the LORD, and
made vows.*

Jonah's presence onboard,
And God's interaction with him,
Was enough to provoke mariners, though
   ignorant of the true God,
To sacrifice and vow to Yahweh.

Would this become a pattern?

Jonah certainly didn't board the ship
Intending an evangelistic campaign!

RETURN

The Fish

Now the LORD had prepared a great fish to swallow up Jonah. And Jonah was in the belly of the fish three days and three nights.

The Hebrew word is "fish."

In the New Testament, when Jesus referred
    to this story,
He used the Greek word for
"Sea-monster, whale, huge fish,"
The root word for *Cetacae*,
The modern biological order of
    aquatic mammals.

A large aquatic animal swallowed Jonah.

Engulfed,
Devoured,
Destroyed him.

A Fish

Now the LORD had prepared a great fish to swallow up Jonah. And Jonah was in the belly of the fish three days and three nights.

Yahweh had prepared a fish.

He had

Assigned,
Appointed,
Ordained

This fish.

No coincidence.
Right place, right time.

A Private Submarine

*Now the LORD had prepared a great fish to
swallow up Jonah. And Jonah was in the belly
of the fish three days and three nights.*

As a child, without much understanding
   of anatomy,
I pictured this aquatic animal with a
   partially airy chamber,
Maybe space even for a candle burning for
   some light and orientation.
Whales require air, and so I figured that
   Jonah would have shared the bounty,
Resting comfortably in his private
   submarine,
Purposefully heading back toward shore.

No.

I think the picture looks more like:
Jonah was in the process of drowning.

During those few minutes of being
   dragged down,
The whale gulped his body,
And there he was, inside.

The creation exhibits compact design,
With no convenient man-sized open spaces
   in any being.

Swallowed

Now the LORD had prepared a great fish to swallow up Jonah. And Jonah was in the belly of the fish three days and three nights.

Historically and scientifically speaking,
Occasionally a whale accidentally
   engulfs a person,
Taking it into its enormous mouth.

But most whales have tiny throats,
And spit back out anything large taken in.

Clearly not the case here:
Jonah wasn't in the mouth, but in the belly.
Is this possible?

The blue whale and others have baleen,
   not teeth,
Keratin plates, like a comb,
To strain out water and keep in tiny krill.

Teethed whales eat food.
Of modern animals,[50]
Only sperm whales have a large enough
   esophagus to swallow a man.

Sperm whales usually live in the open ocean,
Almost two miles underwater.[51]

Belly

*Now the LORD had prepared a great fish to
swallow up Jonah. And Jonah was in the belly
of the fish three days and three nights.*

Humans have one stomach.
Cows have four.

Sperm whales have three:
Forestomach, main stomach,
   pyloric stomach.

The forestomach is like a bird's gizzard.
Birds lack teeth, and so they eat
   small stones,
Which go into the gizzard, and there
   grind up food.
Similarly, sperm whales swallow stones
   and shells,
And the forestomach breaks down the food,
A sort of rock-tumbler chewing.

The main stomach secretes hydrochloric acid
And other chemical agents to break
   down food.

The pyloric stomach secretes pyloric acid.

These stomachs connect with narrow
  openings.[52]
Most likely, then, the body of Jonah went
From mouth to esophagus to forestomach.
Ground up, yes.

But was he chemically burned?
Hydrochloric acid is a strong acid.
Even a short time in that stomach would
  leave him terribly disfigured.
If he wasn't already dead, it would kill him.

Three Days and Three Nights

Now the LORD had prepared a great fish to swallow up Jonah. And Jonah was in the belly of the fish three days and three nights.

In Hebrew, "three days" is an idiom,
An expression that doesn't translate well,
With specific meaning for the
    original hearers.

In English, "raining cats and dogs"
    is an idiom,
Meaning "raining hard."
No small mammals fall from the sky.

"Three days" could mean "parts of
    three days."
But not when "and three nights" is added.
"Three days and three nights" means exactly
    what it says.

New Salt

*Now the LORD had prepared a great fish to
swallow up Jonah. And Jonah was in the belly
of the fish three days and three nights.*

Jonah, after losing his saltiness,
Stayed in the belly of the fish
Three days and three nights,
Soaking in a salt water brine.

Like a cucumber
Fermenting to a pickle,
This time left him
Permanently changed.

The Seventh Great

Now the LORD had prepared a great fish to swallow up Jonah. And Jonah was in the belly of the fish three days and three nights.

Great city.
Great wind.
Great tempest.
Great fear.
Great tempest.
Great fear.
Great fish.

Seven is the number of completeness,
As with Christ's seven words on the cross.
It's a number of exoneration—
The Israelites canceled debts every
    seventh year[53]—
And a number of forgiveness,
As Jesus told Peter to forgive not
    seven times,
But seventy times seven.[54]

It's a number of healing,
As Naaman bathed seven times in
    the Jordan.[55]

It's a number of wholeness:
The seven days for full creation.
And a number of rest:
"And on the seventh day God ended his
 work which he had made;
And he rested on the seventh day from all
 his work which he had made."[56]

How many of these words describe Jonah
At this moment in the story?
Completeness, exoneration,
Forgiveness, healing,
Wholeness, rest?
Really, only rest.

Then

Then Jonah prayed unto the LORD his God out of the fish's belly,

Oh, that tricky word "Then."

For years I imagined angry Jonah, wrestling
  with God three days,
Eating occasional raw fish that also found
  their way into the whale's belly,
Somehow avoiding both salt water and
  stomach acid, but still staying hydrated.

Finally he came to his senses.
"Fine! I'll obey!"

Rather, more accurately, this was the
  moment of

Resurrection.

Pray

*Then Jonah prayed unto the LORD his God out
of the fish's belly,*

Think of the disorientation.
Smooshed in a tiny place,
Without air,
Physically pummeled.

From this place,
Jonah prayed
To Yahweh, the true God.

Scripture has many different words
    for "pray,"
But in this case:

Intervene,
Interpose,
Intercede,
Entreat.

To mediate,
Make supplication,
Judge.

He asked on his own behalf.

The Whole Prayer

And said,
I cried by reason of mine affliction unto
   the LORD,
And he heard me;
Out of the belly of hell cried I,
And thou heardest my voice.
For thou hadst cast me into the deep,
In the midst of the seas;
And the floods compassed me about:
All thy billows and thy waves
   passed over me.
Then I said, I am cast out of thy sight;
Yet I will look again toward thy holy temple.
The waters compassed me about, even to
   the soul:
The depth closed me round about,
The weeds were wrapped about my head.
I went down to the bottoms of the
   mountains;
The earth with her bars was about me
   for ever:
Yet hast thou brought up my life from
   corruption, O LORD my God.
When my soul fainted within me I
   remembered the LORD:

And my prayer came in unto thee, into thine holy temple.
They that observe lying vanities forsake their own mercy.
But I will sacrifice unto thee with the voice of thanksgiving;
I will pay that that I have vowed.
Salvation is of the LORD.

The Whole Prayer, Contemporary

In trouble, deep trouble, I prayed to God.
He answered me.
From the belly of the grave I cried, "Help!"
You heard my cry.
You threw me into ocean's depths,
Into a watery grave,
With ocean waves, ocean breakers
Crashing over me.
I said, "I've been thrown away,
Thrown out, out of your sight.
I'll never again lay eyes
On your Holy Temple."
Ocean gripped me by the throat.
The ancient Abyss grabbed me and
  held tight.
My head was all tangled in seaweed
At the bottom of the sea where the
  mountains take root.
I was as far down as a body can go,
And the gates were slamming shut behind
  me forever—
Yet you pulled me up from that grave alive,
O God, my God!
When my life was slipping away,
I remembered God,

And my prayer got through to you,
Made it all the way to your Holy Temple.
Those who worship hollow gods, god-frauds,
Walk away from their only true love.
But I'm worshiping you, God,
Calling out in thanksgiving!
And I'll do what I promised I'd do!
Salvation belongs to God![57]

He Knew His Bible

*And said, I cried by reason of mine affliction
unto the LORD, and he heard me; out
of the belly of hell cried I, and thou
heardest my voice.*

In six of the eight verses of this prayer,
Jonah quoted scripture.

Clearly, he had pursued the things of God
So diligently

That even in the most intense of
   circumstances,
The words of the scripture came to him,

As here, from the Psalms:
"'The cords of death entangled me,

The anguish of the grave came over me;
I was overcome by distress and sorrow.'"[58]

Cried

And said, I cried by reason of mine affliction unto the LORD, and he heard me; out of the belly of hell cried I, and thou heardest my voice.

Jonah was told to cry against Nineveh. Instead, he cried in distress to the Lord.

"I cried in my
Affliction,
Adversity,
Anguish,
Distress,
Tribulation,
Trouble."

If an intense prayer can also be humorous, The literal meaning of "affliction" here is "Tightness."

Yes. The forestomach of a whale
  would, indeed,
Be tight.

Theme and Variation

*And said, I cried by reason of mine affliction
unto the LORD, and he heard me; out
of the belly of hell cried I, and thou
heardest my voice.*

Hebrew poetry does not rely on
 rhythm or rhyme,
Making it uniquely suitable for translation
 into any language.

Rather, Hebrew poetry often presents
 one thought,
Expressed in two slightly different ways.

Jonah uses two different words for "cried,"
And two different words for "heard,"

To emphasize
How attuned are the ears of the LORD.

The noise of the violent storm
Did not prevent Yahweh from hearing.

Jonah's location
Did not prevent Yahweh from hearing.

Jonah cried.
Yahweh heard.

Heard

*And said, I cried by reason of mine affliction
unto the LORD, and he heard me; out
of the belly of hell cried I, and thou
heardest my voice.*

The first word "heard"
Also means "answered."
Heard and answered.

First clause:
I called in my strait place,
And Yahweh heard and answered.

Second clause:
I called for help from the belly of Sheol.

Not the same word for "belly"
Used for "the belly of the whale,"
But "belly" metaphorically,
As the depth of the grave.

Jonah found himself in Sheol,
In the grave, the pit—
In hell—
Crying for help.

Even there, Yahweh
Heard,
Listened to,
Understood,
Heard intelligently

Jonah's voice.

Underwater words are muffled
At the best of times.

And yet ... who is like this God?

Cast

For thou hadst cast me into the deep, in the midst of the seas; and the floods compassed me about: all thy billows and thy waves passed over me.

You had thrown me into the deepest part,
Into the heart of the seas.
The rivers of the sea encircled me.
All the waves and billows,
All the rolling springs,
All the chastisement of Yahweh,
Passed over me, covered me.

From the Psalms:
"Deep calls to deep
In the roar of your waterfalls;
All your waves and breakers
Have swept over me."[59]

Whodunit

For thou hadst cast me into the deep, in the midst of the seas; and the floods compassed me about: all thy billows and thy waves passed over me.

Interesting accusation:
That Yahweh was the one to cast him into the heart of the seas.

Except the mariners obviously did the casting into the deep,
Acting on Jonah's instructions.

Like Adam, blaming not only Eve, but God himself:
"It was the woman you gave me."[60]

And yet ... God did send the storm,
Cutting off options until jettisoning Jonah was the only option left.

God is the Creator and Sustainer, yes.
But his creation acts according to conscience and desire.

Should God really take the blame
For Jonah's rebellion?
And yet ... God did give Jonah unwelcome
instructions.
Just how far back should the blame and
blame-shifting go?

Hear from Heaven, Your Dwelling Place

Then I said, I am cast out of thy sight; yet I will look again toward thy holy temple.

From the Psalms:
"In my alarm I said,
'I am cut off from your sight!'
Yet you heard my cry for mercy
When I called to you for help."[61]

At Solomon's dedication of the Temple,
He asked God:
"Whatever disaster or disease may come,
And when a prayer or plea is made by
   anyone among your people Israel—
Being aware of the afflictions of their
   own hearts,
And spreading out their hands toward
   this temple—
Then hear from heaven, your dwelling place.
Forgive and act; deal with everyone
   according to all they do,
Since you know their hearts (for you alone
   know every human heart)."[62]

Divorced

Then I said, I am cast out of thy sight; yet I will look again toward thy holy temple.

As he sank down, Jonah recognized that he
   was cast out
From God's eyes,
From God's sight.

Expelled,
Driven out,
Put away,
Thrust out,

Divorced.

Yet

Then I said, I am cast out of thy sight; yet I will look again toward thy holy temple.

Nevertheless.
Notwithstanding.
Surely.
Truly.
Certainly.

But.

That is not the end of the story.

Look Again

Then I said, I am cast out of thy sight; yet I will look again toward thy holy temple.

I may be in the depths of the grave,
But I will look again toward your
　holy temple.

I will look intently,
Regard with pleasure, favor, and care,
Behold,
Consider,
See

Again.

I join myself to,
Add to,
Increase

My looking
Toward

Your temple:
A sacred, dedicated, consecrated, set apart
Sanctuary.

I looked toward Tarshish for a time.
Now I look with pleasure and
　increased regard
Toward your sacred sanctuary.

Compassed

The waters compassed me about, even to the soul: the depth closed me round about, the weeds were wrapped about my head.

From the Psalms:
"Save me, O God,
For the waters have come up to my neck."[63]

Water surrounded me,
Even to my life, my breath, my living being.

The deep, the grave,
Encircled me.

Reeds and seaweeds
Wrapped around my head.

The claustrophobic description of
Drowning,

From one who had been there
And back.

Down and Up

*I went down to the bottoms of the mountains;
the earth with her bars was about me for
ever: yet hast thou brought up my life from
corruption, O LORD my God.*

Earlier, Jonah went
Down to Tarshish,
Down into the ship,
Down into the sides of the ship.

In a fitting punishment,
Now he went down again,
But farther and darker.

Down to the base of the mountains.

The bars of the earth were about him

Perpetually,
For ever and always,
Continuously,
Indefinitely,
To the vanishing point.

And yet, from this nadir,

Yahweh Elohim
Brought up his life from corruption.

No longer the pit, destruction, a trap.

The renewal ascended,
The revival was lifted up.

No matter how far down he went,
Now life came up.

I Remembered

When my soul fainted within me I remembered the LORD: and my prayer came in unto thee, into thine holy temple.

From the Psalms:
"I remembered you, God, and I groaned;
I meditated, and my spirit grew faint."[64]

When my soul drooped,
Grew feeble and faint,

When I was overwhelmed,
  enveloped, covered,

I called to mind,
Was brought to remembrance,
Reminded myself,
Remembered

Yahweh himself.

My prayer—
My supplication, intercession, hymn—

Came

To your holy temple.

Forsake

They that observe lying vanities forsake their own mercy.

An obscure verse.

The five words in Hebrew, in order:

1. Verb: Keep, observe, give heed, regard
2. Noun: Emptiness, vanity, falsehood
3. Adverb: Vainly
4. Verb: Forsake, leave, loose
5. Noun: Lovingkindness

Those who vainly regard falsehoods
Leave lovingkindness.

Had Jonah harbored false ideas of God,
And so forsaken mercy?

Mercy

They that observe lying vanities forsake their own mercy.

The word translated "mercy"
Is the Hebrew word *hesed*, or *chesed*,
Translated elsewhere

Mercy,
Kindness,
Goodness,
Faithfulness,

Lovingkindness.

Loyal-love.
Steadfast-love.
Faithful-love.
Unfailing-love[65]

"Hesed is never merely an abstract feeling of goodwill,
But always entails practical action on behalf of another."[66]

It "intervenes on behalf of loved ones
And comes to their rescue."[67]
How foolish to forsake lovingkindness.

Two Opposite Meanings

They that observe lying vanities forsake their own mercy.

In most cases, the Hebrew word *hesed*
Is translated to mean many lovely words:
Mercy, kindness, goodness, favor, faithfulness.

But on rare occasions it means instead:
A reproach, a shame.

What?
Mercy and shame seem like opposites.

And yet: in the context of correction, or chastisement,
Of wickedness being punished,
Reproach may be a mercy.

Those who heed lying vanities forsake their own correction.

This may have been Jonah at first ...

But no longer.

An Alternative Read

They that observe lying vanities forsake their own mercy.

Figuratively, "falsehood" could be "Idolatry."

Those who vainly give heed to idols
Forsake mercy.

"Those who cling to worthless idols
Turn away from God's love for them."[68]

Perhaps Jonah still protested, just a bit:
The people of Nineveh cling to
   worthless idols!

If Jonah sought to contrast
The rotten people of Nineveh with himself,
What a contrast.

They worship idols,
But *I* sacrifice to you.
Perhaps.

Sacrifice

But I will sacrifice unto thee with the voice of thanksgiving; I will pay that that I have vowed. Salvation is of the LORD.

From the Psalms:
"Salvation belongeth unto the Lord:
Thy blessing is upon thy people. Selah."[69]

I will slaughter an animal as a
 sacrifice to you,
With the sound of thanksgiving, praise,
 and thanks.

I will complete that which I have vowed.
I will be safe in that which I have vowed.
I will render, perform, finish that which I
 have vowed.

Salvation,
Help,
Deliverance,
Health,
Welfare,
Prosperity,

Victory

Is of Yahweh.

Literally:
Yeshua is of Yahweh.

Turn Around

But I will sacrifice unto thee with the voice of thanksgiving; I will pay that that I have vowed. Salvation is of the LORD.

Some commentators note that Jonah never sought forgiveness.
He never said precisely, "I repent."
Especially odd in a book about the need for repentance.

And yet ...
Jonah stopped going in the wrong direction
And turned back to his starting place.

Perhaps not repentance as a spoken declaration,
But the evidence of a life literally
Turned around.

It's the start of a beginning, again.

The Sign of Jonah

*And the LORD spake unto the fish, and it
vomited out Jonah upon the dry land.*

In Jesus' day,
The Pharisees and teachers of the law
 said to him,
"Teacher, we want to see a sign from you."

"He answered, 'A wicked and adulterous
 generation asks for a sign!
But none will be given it except the sign of
 the prophet Jonah.
For as Jonah was three days and three nights
 in the belly of a huge fish,
So the Son of Man will be three days and
 three nights in the heart of the earth.
The men of Nineveh will stand up at the
 judgment with this generation
And condemn it;
For they repented at the preaching of Jonah,
And now something greater than Jonah
 is here.'"[70]

Jonah was three days and three nights
 in the fish

Before his resurrection.

Jesus was three days and three nights
   in the tomb
Before his resurrection.

Both physical bodies subjected to
   natural decay

Before God's reversal.

Return to Land

*And the LORD spake unto the fish, and it
vomited out Jonah upon the dry land.*

The LORD created the fish, and the sea, and
the dry land.

What did it look like for the LORD to speak
to the fish, to command the fish?
What language do fish speak?
Can they usually vomit on command?

Despite these unanswered questions,
Jonah returned to dry ground.

Perhaps back again to his starting place.

Or perhaps simply back on land,
With the need to somehow arrange
Passage back to the starting point.

OBEDIENCE

The Second Time

And the word of the LORD came unto Jonah the second time, saying,

In the Hebrew, this verse is almost identical to the opening of the book.
The earlier verse read:
"Now the word of the LORD came unto Jonah the son of Amittai, saying"—

Simply swap "the son of Amittai" for "the second time."
Back to the beginning,

Again.

Shift

*Arise, go unto Nineveh, that great city, and
preach unto it the preaching that I bid thee.*

As at the first,
The Hebrew begins with these two verbs:
Arise!
Go!

Rise up, stand up, get up!
Go! Walk!

To Nineveh, that great city,
A city proud, large, important, haughty,
    insolent.[71]

And cry, call, proclaim:
In Hebrew, the verb *qara*.

But here the invitation shifted.

No longer a message about the city's
    wickedness
Coming before the Yahweh's faces.

Now Jonah was to cry, call, proclaim

The noun made from the Hebrew *qara*.

Cry the crying,
Call the calling,
Proclaim the proclaiming
Toward her
That I am speaking to you.

The Eighth Great

*Arise, go unto Nineveh, that great city, and
preach unto it the preaching that I bid thee.*

The great fish was the seventh great.
Here we have the eighth great,
The same again as the first: that great city.

The number eight is the number of:

Resurrection,
As the day Jesus rose from the dead;

Regeneration,
As the start of a new week
Or a new octave, or a new rainbow.

A new beginning.
A commencement.

Amen. So be it.

Arise, Again

So Jonah arose, and went unto Nineveh, according to the word of the LORD. Now Nineveh was an exceeding great city of three days' journey.

In the Hebrew, the connection is clear.

The LORD said: Arise, go to Nineveh.
Qum yalak el Nineveh.

Jonah did
Arise.

This time he also
Went

To the proper city.
Qum yalak el Nineveh.

He arose and went to Nineveh,
According to the word of the LORD.

Another Arise

So Jonah arose, and went unto Nineveh, according to the word of the LORD. Now Nineveh was an exceeding great city of three days' journey.

Hundreds of years later,
Jesus went to the bed of Jairus' daughter.
She had died while he was on the way,
And yet he spoke to her:

"*Talitha koum!*"
"Little girl, I say to you, 'Get up!'"[72]

That same word, *qum* in Hebrew, "Arise,"
To another one who was dead,

Now alive.

Arise.

No Crybaby Here

So Jonah arose, and went unto Nineveh, according to the word of the LORD. Now Nineveh was an exceeding great city of three days' journey.

Even though Jonah may have been
   physically marred
From his experience with the LORD and
   with the whale,

He didn't waste a single bit of the
   story saying,
"Woe is me. Look how painful it is to be in
   the hands of a living God."

Not a crybaby.
He just dealt with it.

Like Job: "The Lord gave and the Lord has
   taken away;
May the name of the Lord be praised."[73]

Exceeding Great

So Jonah arose, and went unto Nineveh, according to the word of the LORD. Now Nineveh was an exceeding great city of three days' journey.

Ancient historians Diodorus Siculus
   and Herodotus
Both wrote that Nineveh was about sixty
   miles in circumference,
About twenty miles across.

"Such cities included large areas
For cultivation and pasturage."[74]

Indeed, a great city.

Three Days' Journey

*So Jonah arose, and went unto Nineveh,
according to the word of the LORD. Now
Nineveh was an exceeding great city of three
days' journey.*

I have, on occasion, walked a
   marathon in a day,
Sustained by quick snack foods and
   nice trails.
I asked my backpacker husband how far he
   would walk
When laden with twenty percent of his
   body weight,
Carrying all camping, sleeping, eating, and
   clothing supplies.
"About six or eight miles.
But we weren't usually training in advance."

A three days' walk, indeed, in the Middle
   Eastern sun.

The Ninth Great

So Jonah arose, and went unto Nineveh, according to the word of the LORD. Now Nineveh was an exceeding great city of three days' journey.

The number nine is associated
with judgment.

In this ninth use of the word "great,"

The message of judgment arrived
in Nineveh.

An exceeding great city.

Exceeding

So Jonah arose, and went unto Nineveh, according to the word of the LORD. Now Nineveh was an exceeding great city of three days' journey.

In the Hebrew:
"Nineveh was a great city to Elohim, Three days' walk."

The word "exceeding"
Is the word "Elohim."

Of the 2,606 times the scripture uses this word,
This is the only time it is translated "exceeding,"
Though twice it is translated "mighty,"
And twice it is translated "great."

By contrast, 2,346 times it is translated "God,"
And another 244 times it is translated "god."

It is a plural word used for the singular "God."

Now Nineveh was a god's great city.
Now Nineveh was God's great city.

The one true God thought of this as a great city.

He also cared about it.

Greatly.

And So He Began

And Jonah began to enter into the city a day's journey, and he cried, and said, Yet forty days, and Nineveh shall be overthrown.

Jonah began
Like an opening wedge,
Piercing, boring a hole,

Creating a space
For a message
Where none was before.

Forty

*And Jonah began to enter into the city a day's
 journey, and he cried, and said, Yet forty days,
 and Nineveh shall be overthrown.*

Jonah entered the city,
Went a day's journey,
And he cried, called, proclaimed.

"Only forty more days,
And Nineveh will be overthrown."

Forty. The number of probation, of
"Divine order applied to earthly things."[75]

All that was out of order in the city
Would soon be put right.

Overthrown

And Jonah began to enter into the city a day's journey, and he cried, and said, Yet forty days, and Nineveh shall be overthrown.

In forty days,
Nineveh shall be
Overthrown,

Overturned,
Turned over,
Turned around,

Transformed,
Reversed,
Converted.

Why Did This Message Work?

> *So the people of Nineveh believed God, and proclaimed a fast, and put on sackcloth, from the greatest of them even to the least of them.*

Improbably,
The single sentence sermon
Prompted real change.

The foreigner came to proclaim,
"Yet forty days, and Nineveh shall be overthrown"...
And the people believed God.

Why?

Scathed

*So the people of Nineveh believed God, and
proclaimed a fast, and put on sackcloth, from
the greatest of them even to the least of them.*

Presumably,
Jonah did not escape unscathed
From the belly of the whale.

Imagine skin entirely burned by acid,
Digits eaten away,
Bones broken and mended imperfectly.

Imagine a living zombie,
Damaged and grotesque,
Walking a day's journey into a great city.

Plenty of time to attract a curious, horrified
  following,
Willing to believe
When he announced the coming judgment.

God Uses It All

So the people of Nineveh believed God, and proclaimed a fast, and put on sackcloth, from the greatest of them even to the least of them.

If this interpretation is correct,
Then Jonah's very flight was necessary
To make his message believable.

God can use everything.

Even our rebellion.

Believed

So the people of Nineveh believed God, and proclaimed a fast, and put on sackcloth, from the greatest of them even to the least of them.

The people of Nineveh believed Elohim.

The scripture doesn't say that they
   believed *Jonah*,
Though he was the mouthpiece of God.

They trusted that *God* was able to do
The promised overturning.

Desperation

So the people of Nineveh believed God, and proclaimed a fast, and put on sackcloth, from the greatest of them even to the least of them.

A professor in ancient history calculated
That at exactly this time,
Assyrian history was "shrouded in darkness for forty years."
The neighboring countries began to assert independence.[76]

The Assyrians must have realized that their nation was in trouble.
Desperation prompted change.

The Next Proclamation

So the people of Nineveh believed God, and proclaimed a fast, and put on sackcloth, from the greatest of them even to the least of them.

Jonah
Cried,
Called,
Proclaimed
His message.

In response,
The people of Nineveh
Cried,
Called,
Proclaimed
A fast.

How to placate an angry deity?
The Hebrews, the Persians, the Greeks,
And even Alexander the Great
All, at times, abstained from food in religious observance.[77]

A way to amplify the prayer:
"Help, Lord!"

Sackcloth

*So the people of Nineveh believed God, and
proclaimed a fast, and put on sackcloth, from
the greatest of them even to the least of them.*

"Sackcloth" is the same word for "sack."
The people of Nineveh clothed
    themselves in sacks,
Loosely woven bags of rough material.

A constant skin irritant.

The scripture first uses this word when
    Jacob heard that
His beloved son Joseph was dead.
He clothed himself in sacks,
A way for his outer self to match
The pain of his inner self.

Think of the sense of gnawing hunger
    from fasting.
Think of the perpetual torment of rough
    textiles on the skin.

Let the outer pain seek to regulate the inner
    affliction.

The Tenth Great

So the people of Nineveh believed God, and proclaimed a fast, and put on sackcloth, from the greatest of them even to the least of them.

All participated, from the greatest to the least.
From the oldest to the youngest,
From the largest to the smallest,
From the most important to the least significant.

The tenth "great" in the book,
The number of perfection.

Another number of new beginnings,
As the digits change from single to double.

What hope for the miserable Ninevites:
Change was coming.

Even Unto the King

For word came unto the king of Nineveh, and
he arose from his throne, and he laid his robe
from him, and covered him with sackcloth, and
sat in ashes.

The word didn't just *come* to the king
  of Nineveh,
A casual message delivered and soon
  forgotten.

The word *touched* the king of Nineveh.
It laid its hands upon him,
It struck him violently.

This word *naga* in Hebrew
Is also a euphemism for intercourse
  with a woman.

This word did not leave the king unchanged.

Arose

For word came unto the king of Nineveh, and he arose from his throne, and he laid his robe from him, and covered him with sackcloth, and sat in ashes.

Jonah arose and went the wrong way
Before he arose and went the right way.

Here the king arose from his throne,
He arose from his seat of power and
  authority,

And he set aside his robe,
His glory, his mantle.

In humility, he covered himself
With sackcloth,

And sat, not on a throne,
But in ashes.

He overturned his own expressions of power
To take on the expressions of grief and
  desperation.

Ashes

*For word came unto the king of Nineveh, and
he arose from his throne, and he laid his robe
from him, and covered him with sackcloth, and
sat in ashes.*

Think of the reality of ashes.
Wood, burned up.
Its usefulness gone.
Powdery dust that gets onto and into
 everything.
An irritant.
A sign of despair, of grief.
The opposite of a flourishing green tree.

Sat

For word came unto the king of Nineveh, and
he arose from his throne, and he laid his robe
from him, and covered him with sackcloth, and
sat in ashes.

The Hebrew word for "sat,"
Yasab,
Is not a casual, temporary perch.

It's also translated
"Dwell, remain, abide."

The king made the ashes his dwelling.

Sackcloth and Ashes

For word came unto the king of Nineveh, and he arose from his throne, and he laid his robe from him, and covered him with sackcloth, and sat in ashes.

In the scripture, the phrase "sackcloth and ashes" shows up only occasionally.

When Mordecai heard of Haman's intended destruction,
He put on sackcloth and covered himself with ashes.
So, then, did many other Jews throughout Persia.[78]

Isaiah mocked those who fasted without heart change:
"Is such the fast that I choose,
A day for a person to humble himself?
Is it to bow down his head like a reed,
And to spread sackcloth and ashes under him?
Will you call this a fast,
And a day acceptable to the LORD?"[79]
As if an external performance would

move the heart
Of the God who knows all hearts.

Jeremiah told the unrepentant people of
   Judah to repent.
"Put on sackcloth, my people,
And roll in ashes;
Mourn with bitter wailing as for an
   only son,
For suddenly the destroyer will come
   upon us."[80]

Daniel, too, when he realized that the 70
   years of exile was almost ended:
"So I turned to the Lord God
And pleaded with him in prayer and
   petition,
In fasting,
And in sackcloth and ashes."[81]

All children of Israel ...

And one pagan king,
The king of Nineveh.

A Cry for Help, Again

And he caused it to be proclaimed and published through Nineveh by the decree of the king and his nobles, saying, Let neither man nor beast, herd nor flock, taste any thing: let them not feed, nor drink water:

The king caused this message to be
 "proclaimed,"
The same word used of the mariners,
When they "cried every man unto his god."

A cry for help,
A shriek from anguish or danger.
And sometimes a herald's public
 proclamation.

The king aligned with the mariners
In his absolute understanding of his need,
In his absolute desperation for help.

An Echo of an Earlier Cry for Help

> *And he caused it to be proclaimed and published through Nineveh by the decree of the king and his nobles, saying, Let neither man nor beast, herd nor flock, taste any thing: let them not feed, nor drink water:*

Remember:

"And it came to pass in process of time,
That the king of Egypt died:
And the children of Israel sighed by reason
  of the bondage,
And they cried,
And their cry came up unto God by reason
  of the bondage.
And God heard their groaning,
And God remembered his covenant
With Abraham,
With Isaac, and
With Jacob."[82]

God heard the cry for help out of Egypt.
He remembered his covenant with the
  Patriarchs.

He heard the cry for help out of the
   Mediterranean,
Even with a group of people who had
   no covenant
And didn't even know his name.

Would he hear the cry for help out
   of Nineveh?
Even with a group of people not
   just ignorant,
But vicious?

Just what cries for help would God hear?

Extreme Fast

And he caused it to be proclaimed and published through Nineveh by the decree of the king and his nobles, saying, Let neither man nor beast, herd nor flock, taste any thing: let them not feed, nor drink water:

He commanded that throughout Nineveh,
None should taste anything.

Neither man,
Nor cattle herds,
Nor cow-calf pairs and oxen,
Nor sheep and goats.

No domesticated animal, and no human.
Taste nothing.

Not a speck.

Don't let them graze or feed.
Don't let them drink water.

Clearly this would not be
   sustainable for long—
Animals die quickly in the Middle Eastern

heat without water,
And humans don't last much longer.

But the king was determined:
If there was a way to stave off the
   overturning,
He would find it.

If at all possible,
It would not come on his watch.

The Eleventh Great

And he caused it to be proclaimed and published through Nineveh by the decree of the king and his nobles, saying, Let neither man nor beast, herd nor flock, taste any thing: let them not feed, nor drink water:

The eleventh "great" is not obvious
in English,
Disguised as the word "nobles."

The king and his great ones sent out the
call to fast.

The number eleven may be a number of
disorder and disorganization.[83]
Think of the eleven brothers, left with
despondent Jacob, while Joseph
was in Egypt.
Think of the eleven disciples after the death
of Judas: a chaotic time.

That works here, certainly:
Appropriate enough, as Nineveh was in
an uproar.

But eleven might also be the number of transition.[84]

The eleventh hour is the last possible time—but it is still possible.

Instead

But let man and beast be covered with sackcloth, and cry mightily unto God: yea, let them turn every one from his evil way, and from the violence that is in their hands.

By the king's decree:
Not just the people must cover themselves
    with sackcloth ...
But the animals, too.

Call forcefully, vehemently, strongly
To Elohim.

Turn back from the evil road,
The wicked way,
The malicious course,

And turn back from the violence, the
    wrongs, the cruelty, the injustice
You hold in your palms.

Turn your hand over and empty out
All the evil.

What Is Up with the Cattle?

> But let man and beast be covered with sackcloth, and cry mightily unto God: yea, let them turn every one from his evil way, and from the violence that is in their hands.

Why do the cattle keep coming up?
Fasting cattle, covered in sackcloth?

Is this story simply satire?
Full of exaggeration to emphasize a point?
A sort of joke that the reader understands to be ridiculous?[85]

Perhaps.

But this seems like a modern western perspective.
The animals also faced death.
Perhaps they, too, would fast to seek their own preservation.

But could they repent to God?
Theologically, these are deep waters.

Of course, Jesus said to his disciples,

"Go into all the world
And preach the gospel to every creature."[86]

Jesus could have said,
"Preach the gospel to every person."

Instead, he used a word that means,
"Anything created,
The sum or aggregate of things created."[87]

Do animals, too, need to hear the gospel?

At the very least,
It seems at least reasonable to read
   this command
As part of an extremely eager and
   enthusiastic repentance.

What king, after all,
Would happily set aside throne and mantle
For sackcloth and ashes,

And command his entire realm to
Neither eat nor drink?

When you're desperate,
Might as well extend the call for repentance
To every creature.

Turn and Turn Alike

Who can tell if God will turn and repent, and turn away from his fierce anger, that we perish not?

The king decreed all these measures,
But he had no guarantee that any
would work.

"Who can tell if God will turn and repent?"

He used the same word for "know" that the
    mariners and Jonah used
When they wanted to know who brought on
    the storm,
And when Jonah knew that it was he who
    brought on the storm.

Who will know, who will be sure, if God
    will turn?
If we turn first, will God turn?
Will God turn to comfort and compassion?
    Will he repent?
Will he turn from the fiery fierceness of
    his wrath?

Picture a long-suffering father, finally so fed
   up that he snorts in anger
And moves decisively ...

But is it possible that he hasn't yet had that
   snort of anger?

If God doesn't turn, we will

Perish,
Vanish,
Be destroyed.

Plaintive

Who can tell if God will turn and repent, and turn away from his fierce anger, that we perish not?

Perhaps one man could tell
If God would turn and repent—

But Jonah wasn't telling.

Unknown

Who can tell if God will turn and repent, and turn away from his fierce anger, that we perish not?

God had earlier spoken to Solomon,
On the day that king dedicated the
   temple to God:
"If my people, who are called by my name,
Will humble themselves and pray
And seek my face and turn from their
   wicked ways,
Then I will hear from heaven,
And I will forgive their sin and will heal
   their land."[88]

On the surface, this would indicate that
   repentance bears good fruit.
Except ... this was a promise made to the
   children of Israel.

Would it work for everyone, everywhere?

Repentance

*And God saw their works, that they turned from
their evil way; and God repented of the evil,
that he had said that he would do unto them;
and he did it not.*

Elohim saw the works of the people
   of Nineveh.
They turned back from their evil road.

And so God had compassion,
And did not do the evil that he had said
   he would do.

Fulfillment

And God saw their works, that they turned from their evil way; and God repented of the evil, that he had said that he would do unto them; and he did it not.

Jonah's proclamation:
In forty days,
Nineveh will be
Overthrown,
Overturned,
Turned over,
Turned around,
Transformed,
Reversed,
Converted.

And so his prophecy was
Entirely brought to pass,

But in a completely different way
Than expected.

It was not destroyed, but

Transformed,
Reversed,
Converted.

RESPONSE

Displeased

But it displeased Jonah exceedingly, and he was very angry.

The word "displeased"
Means, literally,
"Breaking to pieces."

He wasn't just unhappy or upset.
He was

Shattered.

Think of the bitterness of
The worst disappointment you've faced—

The broken heart,
The feeling that you've been ground
   into dust.

"Not the waywardness of a child,
But the displeasure of a man of God,
For great and sufficient reason to him.
Now that Nineveh was spared,
It might after all be used as God's rod
   for Israel,
And thus destroy the hope held out by him
   to Israel."[89]

The Twelfth Great

But it displeased Jonah exceedingly, and he was very angry.

God's forbearance
Shattered Jonah

Greatly.

But twelve is the number of
Governmental perfection.
The twelve tribes of Israel.
The twelve disciples of Jesus.

Shouldn't this be a moment of richness,
Of goodness and completion?

Yet it's not.

Perhaps this shows
That God's forbearance
Can, indeed, be shattering.

A human response

To a God-sized grace.

Fury

But it displeased Jonah exceedingly, and he was very angry.

Have no delusion that God can't handle your emotion.

When Jonah was "very angry,"
He was

Furious,
Incensed,
Blazed up in anger.

He had heated himself in vexation.

The forbearance of God vexed Jonah,
And he was crackling with fury.

Stay in Relationship

And he prayed unto the LORD, and said, I pray thee, O LORD, was not this my saying, when I was yet in my country? Therefore I fled before unto Tarshish: for I knew that thou art a gracious God, and merciful, slow to anger, and of great kindness, and repentest thee of the evil.

In his fury,
Jonah did not flee *from* God,

But brought his anger *to* God.
He stayed in relationship with the LORD.

I Told You So

And he prayed unto the LORD, and said, I pray thee, O LORD, was not this my saying, when I was yet in my country? Therefore I fled before unto Tarshish: for I knew that thou art a gracious God, and merciful, slow to anger, and of great kindness, and repentest thee of the evil.

Jonah said,
"I beseech you, Yahweh—
I implore, entreat you—
Didn't I say this,
Back in my own land?

This is why I fled to Tarshish.

I knew your character,
And I believed what you said about yourself.

I knew you'd repent
And not bring destruction
On the destructive ones."

Authorship

And he prayed unto the LORD, and said, I pray thee, O LORD, was not this my saying, when I was yet in my country? Therefore I fled before unto Tarshish: for I knew that thou art a gracious God, and merciful, slow to anger, and of great kindness, and repentest thee of the evil.

Just to clear up any doubt about the identity of the storyteller:
Only Jonah could have accurately told his own internal motivations.

The Most-Quoted Scripture in the Scripture

And he prayed unto the LORD, and said, I pray thee, O LORD, was not this my saying, when I was yet in my country? Therefore I fled before unto Tarshish: for I knew that thou art a gracious God, and merciful, slow to anger, and of great kindness, and repentest thee of the evil.

"Then the LORD came down in the cloud
And stood there with him
And proclaimed his name, the LORD.

And he passed in front of Moses,
Proclaiming,
'The LORD, the LORD,
The compassionate and gracious God,
Slow to anger,
Abounding in love and faithfulness,
Maintaining love to thousands,
And forgiving wickedness, rebellion and sin.
Yet he does not leave the guilty unpunished;
He punishes the children and their children
For the sin of the parents
To the third and fourth generation.'"[90]

This is God's name,
His identity.[91]

Good

Therefore now, O LORD, take, I beseech thee,
   my life from me; for it is better for me to die
   than to live.

I am asking, Yahweh,
That you take the living, enlivened
   part of me.

During your creation, you said over and over
That it was good.

I am overturning that statement,
To say: it is more good for me to die
Than live.

Limited

*Therefore now, O LORD, take, I beseech thee,
my life from me; for it is better for me to die
than to live.*

On the surface, Jonah's statement sounds
   like sour grapes.
A grumpy man, eager for judgment,
Who, like a petulant toddler,
Throws a tantrum because he can't have
   his own way.

Perhaps.

But think of it from the perspective of
   the prophet:
He could have known that judgment
   was coming
And would not be turned aside.

Perhaps he could see his homeland's
   destruction,
The evil brought upon his neighbors and his
   own household.

In this space of shatteredness,

Of grief so deep he didn't see a way forward,
He asked for relief.

And this emotional agony doesn't take
 into account
Whatever physical agony he might
 still endure:
Pain from skin burns, pain from
 crushed bones.

Perhaps not so much petulance
As a very real limit on what anyone
 can endure.

Enter In More Deeply

*Therefore now, O LORD, take, I beseech thee,
my life from me; for it is better for me to die
than to live.*

Hitler died on April 30, 1945.
Berlin fell to the Russians two days later.

In the years to come, various Nazis were
brought to trial.
All of this feels just.

Now imagine, though,
An alternative story.

In mid-March, a Jew, having had a forceful
invitation
To go to Berlin and preach
repentance, began.

When he did,
The city repented.

Hitler told all the people
To fast and pray.

In the next few days,
The Russians turned back.

All the Royal Air Force and American
  planes were grounded.
The global conflagration ended.

Hitler continued his rule, but dismantled
  the death camps.
Mengele, the Angel of Death, retired to
  Argentina.

Oh—and the pesky question of what
  to do with
All the displaced Jews who fled to Palestine?

A German plane carrying a stray
  atomic bomb
Accidentally detonated precisely on
  Jerusalem.

Oh, well.

Israel was never established,
Thanks to the Jew who brought the message
  of repentance.

This is something like the story of Jonah.

Seems like "very angry" would be a
  reasonable response.

Heroes and Anti-Heroes

*Therefore now, O LORD, take, I beseech thee,
my life from me; for it is better for me to die
than to live.*

Dietrich Bonhoeffer,
Pastor, dissident, and attempted
   Hitler assassin,
Seems like the right kind of action-taker.
Thoughtful. Forceful.
He stood up to the Nazis, and they
   executed him.
We celebrate Bonhoeffer.

We have a strong narrative around
Bad guys and good guys in this story.

Now imagine Bonhoeffer going to the Nazis.
Hitler and Goebbels and the others changed
   clothes for a few days,
Promised things would be different.

Should we celebrate that they would go free?

Right and wrong go topsy-turvy.

We crave justice.

Which isn't bad!

Scripture says that righteousness
And justice
Are the foundation of God's throne.[92]

Jonah's response was not bad,
But natural, normal, recognizable.

The book holds a mirror up to our own lives.
Not always comfortable to see.

Challenging

Therefore now, O LORD, take, I beseech thee, my life from me; for it is better for me to die than to live.

What was wrong with Jonah?
Why do we not want to imitate him?
God talked to him, and he heard
   God clearly.
He understood God's character.
He knew the scriptures thoroughly.
He was honest.
And he loved his fellow Israelites!
Doesn't he have it all together?
And yet:
Although he knows God's character,
He doesn't like God's character.
Although he likes his neighbor Israelites,
He doesn't like their enemies.

Lord, may we both know you,
And like you,
Receiving your grace
Both for ourselves and those around us.

A Question

*Then said the LORD, Doest thou well
to be angry?*

Yahweh asked Jonah a question,
But what exactly was he asking?

Probably not an obvious question, like:
"Are you really so very angry?"[93]
"Art thou very much grieved?"[94]

Jonah clearly was very angry.

Also not a binary yes/no question:
"Do you have a good reason to be angry?"[95]

Yes, the coming destruction of an
 entire people
Offered good reason to be angry.

Also probably not:
"Does being angry make you right?"[96]

An emotion is simply an emotion, not
 an argument.
Anger does not make someone right nor

wrong, honorable nor dishonorable.

So is Yahweh asking whether Jonah's anger
   was justified?
"Is it right for you to be angry?"[97]
"Have you any right to be angry?"[98]
"What right do you have to be angry?"[99]

This would be sort of like the answer to Job:
Did you create the world?
Are you God, that you get to dictate
   what happens?
A reasonable question ...
But perhaps there's more.

Perhaps Yahweh was after Jonah's heart:
"Is doing good displeasing to you?"[100]

Like the question Jesus posed in one of
   his parables,
Where the men who worked a full day
   received a day's wages,
And the men who worked an hour received
   a day's wages, too.

When the full-day workers grumbled,
The man who hired them asked,
"Don't I have the right to do what I want
   with my own money?
Or are you envious because I am
   generous?"[101]

Does my character offend you?

Questions to ponder.

And yet ...

Doest Thou Well to Be Angry?

*Then said the LORD, Doest thou well
to be angry?*

"Do you do well to be angry?"[102]

In the Hebrew, this question has two words:
Yatab hara.

Yatab means "to make well, literally or
figuratively."

To make
Sound,
Beautiful,
Happy,
Successful,
Right.

To
Be accepted,
Amend,
Use aright,
Benefit,
Make better,
Seem best,

Make cheerful,
Be comely,
Be content,
Find favor,
Give,
Be glad,
Do good,
Make merry,
Please well,
Make sweet.

Hara is the word for fury,
Blazed up in anger.

Another possible way to read this question:
"Is your fury making you well?
Is your rage producing beauty,
 happiness, success?
Is your anger helping you to be more whole?"

Conspicuous Absence

So Jonah went out of the city, and sat on the east side of the city, and there made him a booth, and sat under it in the shadow, till he might see what would become of the city.

Jonah gave no answer to the question,
But instead went to wait and watch
For the judgment show
That he suspected was not coming ...

But still wished that it was.

Time to Mull Over

So Jonah went out of the city, and sat on the east side of the city, and there made him a booth, and sat under it in the shadow, till he might see what would become of the city.

The kindness and beauty of the LORD.
He asked a question,

But for the moment, in his grace,
He required no answer.

For the moment, in his grace,
He gave space for Jonah to sit in his anger.

For the moment, in his grace,
Jonah had time to be broken-hearted.

For the moment, in his grace,
He left Jonah with a question to consider.

The kindness and beauty of the LORD,
To have patience with this grief-
    stricken man.

Waiting

*So Jonah went out of the city, and sat on the east
side of the city, and there made him a booth,
and sat under it in the shadow, till he might
see what would become of the city.*

Earlier the king sat, or dwelled, in ashes.
Jonah sat, or dwelled, on the east side
 of the city.

A Booth

So Jonah went out of the city, and sat on the east side of the city, and there made him a booth, and sat under it in the shadow, till he might see what would become of the city.

Jonah went out and made himself a
 shelter, a *sukkot*.
As a good Israelite, he would have had
 practice in booth building,
As annually the Israelites constructed
 booths and lived in them for eight days.

The Feast of Tabernacles, the Feast
 of Booths,
This seventh and final annual festival,
A time of thanksgiving for God's provision,
And an invitation to all Israelites to
 remember their wilderness journey.
The eight day booth-dwelling began and
 ended with a sabbath rest,
When all the Israelites were to travel to
 Jerusalem to celebrate together.

Here we find an inverse booth celebration.
Jonah, alone, far from Jerusalem.

Resting, not to think of God's goodness, but
   wishing for God's judgment.
Not thanking God for his gracious
   provision, but wishing for a little less,
Here at the end of his own journey, both to
   the watery ends of the earth,
And to death and back.

The East Side

So Jonah went out of the city, and sat on the east side of the city, and there made him a booth, and sat under it in the shadow, till he might see what would become of the city.

Why give the detail that Jonah sat on the east side?

Metaphorically, "the east side" can mean "that which was before."
Perhaps Jonah was sitting, waiting for the impending judgment,
That which was to come before the people repented.

The first use of this word in the scriptures is this:
"Now the LORD God had planted a garden in the east, in Eden;
And there he put the man he had formed."[103]
Is Jonah subtly saying, "The paradise I want is the place of judgment"?

Or maybe he is thinking of the next use of

the word "east":
"After he drove the man out,
He placed on the east side of the
   Garden of Eden
Cherubim and a flaming sword flashing
   back and forth
To guard the way to the tree of life."[104]

Perhaps he wanted to remind God that God has always been a God of justice?

The Shadow

So Jonah went out of the city, and sat on the east side of the city, and there made him a booth, and sat under it in the shadow, till he might see what would become of the city.

Jonah sat in the shadow of the booth
He made for himself.

But scripture offers many better, more
 beautiful uses of this word
"Shadow" or "shade."

"Keep me as the apple of your eye;
Hide me in the shadow of your wings."[105]

"Whoever dwells in the shelter of
 the Most High
Will rest in the shadow of the Almighty."[106]

"The Lord watches over you—
The Lord is your shade at your
 right hand."[107]

"Like an apple tree among the trees of
 the forest

Is my beloved among the young men.
I delight to sit in his shade,
And his fruit is sweet to my taste."[108]

"He made my mouth like a sharpened sword,
In the shadow of his hand he hid me;
He made me into a polished arrow
And concealed me in his quiver."[109]

Jonah made a shadow for himself,
But the Lord offers a better shadow.

GRACE

Gourd

And the LORD God prepared a gourd, and made it to come up over Jonah, that it might be a shadow over his head, to deliver him from his grief. So Jonah was exceeding glad of the gourd.

Yahweh Elohim had prepared a gourd.

He had

Assigned,
Appointed,
Ordained

This gourd.

No coincidence.
Right place, right time.

Cover

And the LORD God prepared a gourd, and made it to come up over Jonah, that it might be a shadow over his head, to deliver him from his grief. So Jonah was exceeding glad of the gourd.

The fish swallowed Jonah.
The gourd simply covered him.

Picture This

And the LORD God prepared a gourd, and made it to come up over Jonah, that it might be a shadow over his head, to deliver him from his grief. So Jonah was exceeding glad of the gourd.

Imagine Jonah's melted skin,
Now under the Middle Eastern sun,
Sunburned. Tormented.

Imagine his warped fingers,
Seeking to put up a booth in the desert.
Frustrated. Furious.

Now, after this long and intense string
Of frustrations, disappointments, griefs,
At last!

A personal grace.
A gift of God.
Relief.

The Thirteenth Great

And the LORD God prepared a gourd, and made it to come up over Jonah, that it might be a shadow over his head, to deliver him from his grief. So Jonah was exceeding glad of the gourd.

The thirteenth use of the word great in the
 book of Jonah,
Here translated "exceeding."

Thirteen is the number of rebellion and
 disintegration.
Appropriate enough.

And yet the grace comes to Jonah
In the midst of his rebellion.

Great Rejoicing

And the LORD God prepared a gourd, and made it to come up over Jonah, that it might be a shadow over his head, to deliver him from his grief. So Jonah was exceeding glad of the gourd.

To say, "Jonah was exceeding glad of
 the gourd"
Starts to touch on the amount of
 his gladness.
Another translation: "Jonah rejoiced with
 great rejoicing."[110]

In the Hebrew, not only do we find the
 word *gadol,*
"Great, exceeding."

But we also find not one, but two, words for
 happiness.

One, *samah:*
To brighten up,
Make blithe or gleesome,
Cheer up, make glad,
Make joyful, make merry,
Cause to rejoice.

The other, *simha*:
Joy, mirth, gladness,
Gaiety, pleasure, rejoicing.

The Hebrew literally reads:
"He is rejoicing Jonah over the gourd, rejoicing great." [111]

Pile up the happiness words, and add an "exceeding!"

At Last

And the LORD God prepared a gourd, and made it to come up over Jonah, that it might be a shadow over his head, to deliver him from his grief. So Jonah was exceeding glad of the gourd.

Imagine the sigh of relief.
A few stunted branches hardly offered much
    protection.
Did the vine emerge from the ground in
    the night,
Or was Jonah awake when it first poked out?
Did he watch it climb up the side of the
    booth with interest,
Chuckling over how he could see it grow,
Astonished at the large, luscious leaves,
Each one offering dinner-plate sized shade?

After fear, disappointment, grief, distress ...
At last he's caught a break.
At last the universe is bending in his favor ...

At least a little bit.

Over the Top

And the LORD God prepared a gourd, and made it to come up over Jonah, that it might be a shadow over his head, to deliver him from his grief. So Jonah was exceeding glad of the gourd.

From the space of two millennia,
Does the rejoicing seem a bit much?
From shattered to exceeding joy?
Especially over something as
Inconsequential as
A vine?

Perhaps.

And yet ... there is a special type of fatigue
   that sets in at times,
A kind of emotional spent-ness,
In which normal emotional regulation

Vanishes.

How human.
How recognizable.

Intention

And the LORD God prepared a gourd, and made it to come up over Jonah, that it might be a shadow over his head, to deliver him from his grief. So Jonah was exceeding glad of the gourd.

God's intention, here: to deliver him from his grief.
"To ease his discomfort."[112]

The Hebrew word "deliver" means "to snatch away,
Rescue, save, strip, recover."

The word "his grief" means "evil, bad, wickedness,
Adversity, sad, unhappy, miserable, distress, affliction."

The gourd was meant to snatch away his affliction,
To rescue him from his distress,

To recover him from his unhappiness,
To strip him of his misery ... and maybe of his evil, too.

The Evil

And the LORD God prepared a gourd, and made it to come up over Jonah, that it might be a shadow over his head, to deliver him from his grief. So Jonah was exceeding glad of the gourd.

"His grief" is the same word for "evil, wickedness,"
As when God said "their *wickedness* is come up before me,"[113]

Or when the mariners wondered, and then asked,
"For whose cause this *evil* is upon us."[114]

Also when the king told the people,
"Let them turn every one from his *evil* way,"[115]

And twice: "And God saw their works, that they turned from their *evil* way;
And God repented of the *evil*, that he had said that he would do unto them."[116]

The seventh use was embedded in the phrase,

"But it displeased Jonah exceedingly."[117]
(Not visible in the English, but present nonetheless.)

And the eighth when he protested,
"I knew that thou art a gracious God ...
And repentest thee of the *evil*."[118]

Now at last and finally, the gourd comes to
Deliver him from his grief, his distress.

The ninth use.
The number nine is associated
  with judgment.

A Worm

But God prepared a worm when the morning rose the next day, and it smote the gourd that it withered.

Elohim had prepared a worm.

He had

Assigned,
Appointed,
Ordained

This worm.

No coincidence.
Right place, right time.

Every Morning

But God prepared a worm when the morning rose the next day, and it smote the gourd that it withered.

Scripture tells us,
"Because of the LORD's great love
We are not consumed,
For his compassions never fail.

They are new every morning;
Great is your faithfulness."[119]

Jonah had rejoiced with exceeding joy
    at the vine.

Now, in the new day,
God's compassions did not fail.

Even if it seemed, in that moment,
    like they did.

Smitten of God, and Afflicted

But God prepared a worm when the morning rose the next day, and it smote the gourd that it withered.

The worm "smote" the gourd.

The same verb Isaiah used in a prophecy of Jesus.
"Surely He has borne our griefs
And carried our sorrows;

Yet we esteemed Him stricken,
Smitten by God, and afflicted."[120]

Or: "Yet it was our weaknesses he carried;
It was our sorrows that weighed him down.
And we thought his troubles were a punishment from God,
A punishment for his own sins!"[121]

Jesus was smitten, but he wasn't being punished for his sins.
Nor was Jonah being tormented from capricious indifference.

The surface appeared to show one thing;
The inner reality revealed something quite different.

First Rays

And it came to pass, when the sun did arise, that God prepared a vehement east wind; and the sun beat upon the head of Jonah, that he fainted, and wished in himself to die, and said, It is better for me to die than to live.

"When the sun did arise."

Here, "arise" means "radiate."

In the desert, the first rays of sun
Start to heat the surroundings instantly.
Jonah would have felt that radiation
 intensely,
From that first moment.

A Vehement East Wind

And it came to pass, when the sun did arise, that God prepared a vehement east wind; and the sun beat upon the head of Jonah, that he fainted, and wished in himself to die, and said, It is better for me to die than to live.

Elohim had prepared a vehement east wind.

He had

Assigned,
Appointed,
Ordained

This wind.

No coincidence.
Right place, right time.

About the Vehement East Wind

> *And it came to pass, when the sun did arise, that God prepared a vehement east wind; and the sun beat upon the head of Jonah, that he fainted, and wished in himself to die, and said, It is better for me to die than to live.*

In the Hebrew, the word "vehement" only appears this once.
The root word is "silence,"
Which doesn't make much sense, as what kind of intense wind is silent?

Think: "deafening."[122]

So loud, you might as well be deaf.

The word "east" is not the same as the word "east" where Jonah sat.
This "east" refers specifically to the genesis of the wind.
Think "sirocco," the violent east wind of the desert.

As perhaps befits a desert-dwelling people,
The Hebrew lexicon lists specific words for

the north, south, and east winds,
And five different words for "whirlwind."

In the desert, wind matters.

But the Hebrew scriptures have only one word for plain "wind."
Ruach.
Also used for spirit, breath,
Holy Spirit.
"The Spirit of God moved upon the face of the waters."[123]

The three words, then, for "vehement east wind":
Deafening, east wind, Spirit.

God had prepared for Jonah, indeed.

Smitten

And it came to pass, when the sun did arise,
   that God prepared a vehement east wind; and
   the sun beat upon the head of Jonah, that he
   fainted, and wished in himself to die, and said,
   It is better for me to die than to live.

Even as the worm smote the vine,
The sun smote Jonah's head.

This head that earlier had seaweed wrapped
   around it,
And a gourd to shield it,
Now smitten by the sun.

Faint

*And it came to pass, when the sun did arise,
that God prepared a vehement east wind; and
the sun beat upon the head of Jonah, that he
fainted, and wished in himself to die, and said,
It is better for me to die than to live.*

The literal meaning of "fainted" is "covered";
The figurative meanings are "to be languid"
or "faint."

Perhaps Jonah covered himself in the midst

Of the wind and the sun.

But dehydration and exposure also rapidly
Make a person feel faint.

Better

*And it came to pass, when the sun did arise,
that God prepared a vehement east wind; and
the sun beat upon the head of Jonah, that he
fainted, and wished in himself to die, and said,
It is better for me to die than to live.*

Earlier, Jonah asked God to take his
 life from him.
Now he wished in himself to die.

From prayer to private grief,
With the same refrain: "It is better for me to
 die than to live."

But no longer in conversation with God.
His disappointment now was absolute.

Same Question

And God said to Jonah, Doest thou well to be angry for the gourd? And he said, I do well to be angry, even unto death.

Jonah no longer prayed,
But God continued to engage.

God came again with the same question ...
But not the same question.

Earlier he asked, "Do you do well to
 be angry?"
And Jonah didn't reply.

Now God asked again, more specifically:
"Do you do well to be angry *for the plant?*"[124]

This question came as a pressure-release,
As if to say, "I understand that you can't face
Ultimate questions about me and my
 character.

So I'll ask a small-scale question
And see if you'll engage."

Answered

And God said to Jonah, Doest thou well to be angry for the gourd? And he said, I do well to be angry, even unto death.

In his bitterness and anguish,
Jonah answered God.

"Yes.
I do well, even to death."

I Do Well

*And God said to Jonah, Doest thou well to be
angry for the gourd? And he said, I do well to
be angry, even unto death.*

How recognizable, in the midst of a
 deep fury,
To reply to God that the anger is justified.

How inverted, if the question was,
"Is your anger helping you to be
 more whole?"

To reply, "Yes! Even to death!" ...
Which is, of course, the opposite of life and
 wholeness.

The sense of spitting outrage still speaks.
But was Jonah actually doing well?

Compassion

Then said the LORD, Thou hast had pity on the gourd, for the which thou hast not laboured, neither madest it grow; which came up in a night, and perished in a night:

Yahweh's question:
"You had compassion, pity, regard
For this gourd.
You wanted to spare it.

But you didn't toil for it,
You offered no severe and irksome work.

And you didn't make it grow up.

You cared for this plant,
Even though you had nothing to do with it."

Son of the Night

Then said the LORD, Thou hast had pity on the gourd, for the which thou hast not laboured, neither madest it grow; which came up in a night, and perished in a night:

In the Hebrew,
The gourd's description includes the
    word "son."

It was a son of the night,
And perished as a son of the night.

A little personification,
To make a larger point about many persons.

Full Question, Two Ways

Then said the LORD, Thou hast had pity on the gourd, for the which thou hast not laboured, neither madest it grow; which came up in a night, and perished in a night: And should not I spare Nineveh, that great city, wherein are more than sixscore thousand persons that cannot discern between their right hand and their left hand; and also much cattle?

Same passage, contemporary version:

God said, "What's this?
How is it that you can change your feelings
From pleasure to anger
Overnight
About a mere shade tree that you did
  nothing to get?
You neither planted nor watered it.
It grew up one night and died the
  next night.

So, why can't I likewise change what I feel
  about Nineveh
From anger to pleasure,
This big city of more than 120,000

childlike people
Who don't yet know right from wrong,
To say nothing of all the innocent animals?"[125]

Contrast

And should not I spare Nineveh, that great city, wherein are more than sixscore thousand persons that cannot discern between their right hand and their left hand; and also much cattle?

"Jonah, you did not labor, and you did not make grow,
Yet you had compassion and wanted to spare the vine.
Can I not have compassion on this great city?"

The implied contrast here:
"I actually did labor over the plant.
I actually did make it grow.

But more than that,
I also labored over the city.
I actually did make it, too, grow.

My investment is far greater than yours.
The stakes are far higher.
One 'son of the night' plant is small compared to

One hundred twenty thousand people,
Who are ignorant of my ways;
Not to mention all the cattle."

Another Idiom

And should not I spare Nineveh, that great city, wherein are more than sixscore thousand persons that cannot discern between their right hand and their left hand; and also much cattle?

Another expression that carries meaning other than the literal.

The people of Nineveh did not need a
　mass lesson
On which hand is which.

Rather, they were ignorant of good and evil.

The Fourteenth Great

And should not I spare Nineveh, that great city, wherein are more than sixscore thousand persons that cannot discern between their right hand and their left hand; and also much cattle?

Nineveh, that great city.

The fourteenth and final use of the
  word "great."
A double measure of seven,
The number of spiritual perfection,
The number of life,
The number of the work of the
  Holy Spirit.[126]

An ending with an expectation of good.

That Great City

And should not I spare Nineveh, that great city, wherein are more than sixscore thousand persons that cannot discern between their right hand and their left hand; and also much cattle?

I spent a year reading about inner
   city ministry.
Racism. Poverty. Burnout.

I spent months volunteering in the
   inner city.
A child's astonishment at the gift of a
   paperback book.
Complete financial illiteracy: "I bet you
   make $200 a month!"
Toothless meth mom.
A child dropped out of seventh grade.
A middle schooler, tired of being alone, slept
   with fourteen boys in a weekend.
Eighty percent of the girls molested
   by age five.
Broken, broken, broken.

So the idea of the Bible, "It began in a

garden and ends in a city,"
Sounded horrible to me:

Begin in a paradise, tended carefully, filled
 with fruit,

And end in a strip mall with graffiti, an
 enormous parking lot,
And some big box stores across the street,
 accessed only via
Stop lights, always red.

And while I could adjust the vision some—
 this city has streets of gold;
Presumably there would be no sirens or
 rusty rebar,
No burnt-out neon signs and no unhealthy
 fast food—
I still didn't have a heart for the city.

But finally I heard something that
 overturned my understanding.

Start with a garden.
The Creator gives the creation
The gift of co-creation. Trees produce
 more trees.
The world created one day grows and
 develops the next day.
Movement. Transformation.

And we end with a city, which can be
 defined as:

A lot of organized gardens.[127]

Is that not beautiful?

I live on land. Poison ivy, ticks, fallen trees.
But I delight in the beauty when I visit a
   botanic garden, tended, cared for.

And once I visited wealthy community
   Carmel-by-the-Sea,
Where everyone had the means to care for
   their houses and yards.
Walking the streets was a delight:
Each house, each yard, unique and beautiful,
   a reflection of the owners.

Eden: one large, unsubdued garden.
The New Jerusalem: beauty, order,
   responsibility, companionship.
All things in right relationship.

If the city now is fully broken because of the
   mass of broken people,
Think how glorious it will be, with the
   shalom of God
On us all.

No wonder God cared about Nineveh.
No wonder he cares about cities.

Intention Revisited

And should not I spare Nineveh, that great city, wherein are more than sixscore thousand persons that cannot discern between their right hand and their left hand; and also much cattle?

"The LORD God prepared a gourd, ...
To deliver him from his grief,"

To snatch away his affliction,
To rescue him from his distress,

To recover him from his unhappiness,
To strip him of his misery ... and maybe of
 his evil, too.

And at the time, the gourd itself seemed like
 the answer:
A bit of comfort in the midst of a
 tough time.

But that earlier perspective was too limited.
Yahweh Elohim was after far more than
 momentary relief.

To actually strip Jonah of his misery,
Yahweh Elohim had an entire
 performance to enact.

The vine grew, and died;
The man rejoiced, and despaired.

The *vine* wasn't the mechanism to snatch
 away despair;
The *life cycle* of the vine was the mechanism.

The vine would do its work,
Though not in the immediate or
 expected way.

And so the sequence of events
Served to deliver Jonah from his grief ...

If he would be willing.

Open End

And should not I spare Nineveh, that great city, wherein are more than sixscore thousand persons that cannot discern between their right hand and their left hand; and also much cattle?

The book of Jonah ends
Unresolved.

How did Jonah answer God's question?

AFTER

An Educated Guess

With little hints throughout the book about
   Jonah's authorship—
Details of thoughts and prayers,
Not to mention the title—
We can make an educated guess about
   the ending:

Jonah accepted the Lord's rebuke,
And then returned to Israel to write
   his story.

So when he spoke the twice-
   repeated refrain,
"It is better for me to die than to live,"
How lovely to find that, in the end,
He realized: not true.

There was good work yet for him to do.

EPILOGUE

A Realistic Definition of Faithfulness

I love the story of Jonah because he's
   deliciously imperfect
And incredibly honest.

Doesn't it sound good to follow our bliss?
Think of the gorgeous quote by
   Frederick Buechner:
"The place God calls you to
Is the place where your deep gladness
And the world's deep hunger meet."[128]

We *want* that to be true.

And sometimes it is.

But sometimes God calls us to go
   to Nineveh.
To sit at the bedside of a dying wife
   for 109 days.
To walk with a teenager to the gates
   of heaven.
To get up, day by day, and serve the needs of
   a parent with dementia.

Sometimes the call is not nice, but
Awful and
Boring and
Terrifying and
Grievous.
And maybe, in that moment, the
   temptation comes
To look at the normal people and think,
"None of them are called to Nineveh! I don't
   want this call!"

I want a functional marriage!
I want stable mental health for my child!
I want the lies to stop infiltrating the minds
   of my loved ones!
I want my adopted child to be made whole!

For those times when life is hard and tiring,
When nothing around you or in you
   feels joyful,
Jonah delivers good news:

You're not (necessarily) doing
   anything wrong.

Sometimes the call is hard.
Be faithful anyway.

Too Facile

So, in the end, why did I bristle about
The narrative of ethnocentric Jonah?
Because it's too facile, too superficial to say,

"Well, if he just stopped caring only
   about Israel,
Then he wouldn't have found his assignment
   so distasteful."

Of course there is no room for
   ethnocentricity with God,

Who will have people worshipping him

From every nation, tribe, people and
   language.[129]

And we know that Joshua,
When faced with a man with a
   drawn sword,
Asked the commander of the army
   of the LORD,
"Are you for us or for our enemies?"

And the man replied: "Neither."[130]
Because even for his chosen people,
The commander of the army of the LORD

Would not claim to side with the Israelites.

But that's not the complete narrative.

The Prophet for Day-to-Day Trauma

What does it look like to be obedient
When the call of God doesn't look anything
   like what you expect?

When you feel called to adopt, but the child
   doesn't bring more wholeness,
But a fracturing?

When you feel called to farm,
And everything dies?

When you sacrificially go to
   another country,
And find yourself without a visa, and have
   to return home?

When the specific call either goes nothing
   like what you expect,
Or exactly like what you expect, but
   nothing like what you want—

There's weightiness to that.
There's pain to that.

Jonah was never a petulant two year old.
Rather, one who suffered,
  reluctantly faithful.

The prophet for day-to-day trauma.
Constrained to be obedient, but not happy
  about the call.

And even in the midst of the pain,

God is patient, and seeking, and kind, and
  relational.

Faithful God

In the end, we look to God.

The one who worked on behalf of Jonah,
And on behalf of the mariners,
And on behalf of the Ninevites,
Throughout the story, beginning to end.

As he does for us, too.

Thanks be to God.

The End, and the Beginning

"The LORD, the LORD,
The compassionate and gracious God,
Slow to anger,
Abounding in love and faithfulness,
Maintaining love to thousands,
And forgiving wickedness, rebellion and sin.
Yet he does not leave the guilty unpunished;
He punishes the children and their children
For the sin of the parents to the third and
   fourth generation."[131]

Go in peace.

NOTES

1. Genesis, Exodus, Numbers, Deuteronomy, Joshua, I Samuel, II Samuel, I Kings, II Kings, I Chronicles, II Chronicles, Ezra, Psalm, Isaiah, Jeremiah, Ezekiel, Daniel, Hosea, Joel, Amos, Jonah, Micah, Zephaniah, Haggai, Zechariah, Malachi
2. Genesis 15:1
3. Malachi 1:1
4. II Kings 14:23-29 (NIV)
5. I Kings 4:21
6. I Kings 11:23-25
7. Totaling the years of the different rulers: https://jesusalive.cc/kings-israel-judah/. Found 6/5/2022.
8. II Kings 14:26 (NIV)
9. II Kings 14:25
10. John 7:52 (NIV)
11. Note in *The Companion Bible*.
12. https://www.blueletterbible.org/lexicon/h1419/kjv/wlc/0-1/. Found 6/5/2022.
13. In *Thou Shall Prosper*
14. Genesis 10:6-12
15. https://www.britannica.com/place/Nineveh-ancient-city-Iraq. Found 6/11/2022.
16. *God Has a Name*, John Mark Comer, p. 135.
17. Probably Andalusia, Spain.
18. II Chronicles 2:16 and Ezra 3:7, respectively.
19. Note in *The Companion Bible* for Jonah 1:3.
20. From II Kings 14
21. https://www.blueletterbible.org/lexicon/h1419/kjv/wlc/0-1/. Found 6/11/2022.
22. *The Companion Bible*, Appendix 9, p. 13.
23. John 10:10 (NIV)
24. https://www.britannica.com/place/Mediterranean-Sea/Hydrologic-features-and-climate. Found 6/12/2022.
25. Matthew 5:13
26. Genesis 3:10
27. Genesis 18:15
28. Exodus 2:23-24
29. Genesis 12:3
30. Judges 4:21
31. Daniel 8:18, 10:9
32. NIV, Berean Study Bible
33. NASB
34. ESV
35. Literal Standard Version
36. Appendix 44, p. 37
37. Proverbs 16:33 (NIV)
38. Proverbs 16:33 (NLT)
39. Mark 4:39 (NIV)
40. Isaiah 45:7 (NIV)
41. Genesis 2:2
42. *The Companion Bible*, note for II Chronicles 36:23. It also notes all 20 other occurrences: Ezra 1:2, 5:11, 5:12, 6:9, 6:10, 7:12, 7:21,

7:23; Nehemiah 1:4, 1:5, 2:4, 2:20; Psalm 136:26; Daniel 2:18, 2:19, 2:37, 2:44; Jonah 1:9; Revelation 11:13, 16:11.
43 Jonah uses the same words used in the Genesis 1:9-10 creation account for "sea" and "dry land."
44 The Bible Project's *Jonah*: https://www.youtube.com/watch?v=dLl-abZcOO4c&vl=en. Found 6/13/2022.
45 From the computer dictionary definition.
46 https://www.scripture4all.org/OnlineInterlinear/OTpdf/jon1.pdf. Found 6/12/2022.
47 Exodus 20:13 (NIV)
48 *Pinocchio* comes to mind
49 https://www.scripture4all.org/OnlineInterlinear/OTpdf/jon1.pdf. Found 6/12/2022.
50 The obvious statement here is that we don't necessarily know what sea creatures may have existed in the depths several millennia ago. Not much deep sea archaeology happening.
51 https://www.nationalgeographic.com/animals/article/most-whales-cant-really-swallow-a-human-heres-why. Found 6/19/2022.
52 https://whalenutrition.wordpress.com/2015/02/23/digestive-anatomy/. Found 6/19/2022.
53 Deuteronomy 15:1-2
54 Matthew 18:21-22
55 II Kings 5
56 Genesis 2:2
57 Jonah's prayer in Jonah 2 in *The Message*
58 Psalm 116:3 (NIV)
59 Psalm 42:7 (NIV)
60 Genesis 3:12 (TLB)
61 Psalm 31:22 (NIV)
62 I Kings 8:37-39 (NIV)
63 Psalm 69:1 (NIV)
64 Psalm 77:3 (NIV)
65 https://www.christianity.com/wiki/christian-terms/what-is-hesed-love-and-what-does-it-tell-us-about-gods-love-for-us.html. Found 4/6/2022.
66 https://firmisrael.org/learn/the-meaning-of-hesed-hebrew-for-love/, quoting Dr. Will Kynes. Found 4/6/2022.
67 Ibid, quoting Lois Tverberg.
68 Jonah 2:8 (NIV)
69 Psalm 3:8
70 Matthew 12:38-41 (NIV); Luke 11:29-32 is a parallel passage, and Jesus also mentions "the sign of Jonah" in Matthew 16:4.
71 https://www.blueletterbible.org/lexicon/h1419/kjv/wlc/0-1/. Found 6/5/2022.
72 Mark 5:41 (NIV)
73 Job 1:21 (NIV)
74 Note in *The Companion Bible*, Jonah 3:2
75 *The Companion Bible*, appendix 10
76 *The Companion Bible* footnote.
77 *The Companion Bible* footnote.
78 Esther 4:1, 3
79 Isaiah 58:5 (ESV)

80 Jeremiah 26:6 (NIV)
81 Daniel 9:3 (NIV)
82 Exodus 2:23-24
83 *The Companion Bible*, Appendix 10.
84 https://dougaddison.com/2017/08/a-deeper-look-at-the-number-11/. Found July 17, 2022.
85 This is the interpretation of The Bible Project, which offers excellent summaries of the books of the Bible. https://www.youtube.com/watch?v=dLIabZc004c. Found July 17, 2022.
86 Mark 16:15 (NKJV)
87 https://www.blueletterbible.org/lexicon/g2937/kjv/tr/0-1/. Found July 17, 2022.
88 II Chronicles 7:14 (NIV)
89 *The Companion Bible* footnote.
90 Exodus 34:5-7 (NIV)
91 John Mark Comer, in *God Has a Name*, writes, "[I]t's quite possibly **the most quoted passage in the Bible,** by the Bible" (p. 32, emphasis his). His footnote says, "I first heard this from Dr. Gerry Breshears of Western Seminary. He got it from Dr. John Sailhamer, of legendary OT scholar fame. Dr. Tim Mackie calls it 'the John 3v16 of the Hebrew Bible.' Here's the short list of where it's quoted: Numbers 14v18; Psalms 86v15; 103v8; 111v4; 112v4; 145v8; Jeremiah 32v18; Joel 2v13; Jonah 4v2; Nahum 1v3; Nehemiah 9v17, 31; 2 Chronicles 30v9. But what are much harder to quantify are all the allusions to it, for which I lack space in the endnotes. For example, 'love and faithfulness'—first used here—is used hundreds of times in the Bible."
92 Psalm 89:14
93 NET
94 Brenton Septuagint Translation
95 NASB
96 International Standard Version
97 NIV
98 Berean Study Bible
99 Contemporary English Version
100 Literal Standard Version
101 Matthew 20:15 (NIV)
102 ESV
103 Genesis 2:8 (NIV)
104 Genesis 3:24 (NIV)
105 Psalm 17:8 (NIV)
106 Psalm 91:1 (NIV)
107 Psalm 121:5 (NIV)
108 Song of Songs 2:3 (NIV)
109 Isaiah 49:2 (NIV)
110 *The Companion Bible* footnote.
111 https://www.scripture4all.org/OnlineInterlinear/OTpdf/jon4.pdf. Found July 18, 2022.
112 NIV
113 Jonah 1:2
114 Jonah 1:7, 1:8
115 Jonah 3:8
116 Jonah 3:10
117 Jonah 4:1
118 Jonah 4:2

119 Lamentations 3:22-23 (NIV)
120 Isaiah 53:4
121 Isaiah 53:4 (TLB)
122 https://www.scripture4all.org/OnlineInterlinear/OTpdf/jon4.pdf. Found July 19, 2022.
123 Genesis 1:2
124 ESV, emphasis mine; the question "Do you do well to be angry" is identical in the Hebrew.
125 Jonah 4:10-11 (MSG)
126 This, and the other number analyses, found in *The Companion Bible*, appendix 10.
127 This insight from Rob Bell, in his 2012 sermon "Beginning in the Beginning," https://www.youtube.com/watch?v=2CwMOcMDjhc. Watched 11/14/2014.
128 *Wishful Thinking*, "Vocation," p. 119.
129 Revelation 7:9
130 Joshua 5:13-14 (NIV)
131 Exodus 34:6-7 (NIV)

ABOUT THE AUTHOR

A.J. Lykosh loves healing and deliverance.

Her heart's cry comes from the verse, "My people are destroyed for lack of knowledge" (Hosea 4:6). The author of several highly acclaimed books, she seeks to stop the destruction as best she can through writing and speaking. She sends daily emails about prayer, and podcasts at Make Prayer Beautiful.

She loves feedback. Email <u>amy@workplaceprayer.com</u> to start a conversation.

MAKARIOS PRESS

Be in your happy place.

PRAY HEAVEN TO EARTH
Why Workplace Prayer Exists

When Jesus taught on prayer, he began, "Our Father in heaven, hallowed be your name, your kingdom come, your will be done, on earth as it is in heaven." How can we effectively pray God's kingdom on earth, if we don't know what heaven looks like? If we want to pray better, we need to understand what we're praying for. Catch a glimpse of heaven in these short free verse poems, taken from Revelation 4 and 5. Pressed for time? You could read a single chapter. Or even a single poem!

> "I just sat down with your book. I am on the second page. In tears. Thank you. Beautiful and song-like. And fun." — **Sarah**

> "I feel like each line of each poem is like a choice morsel of truth that I just want to savor slowly. I set aside your book to read in quiet and cozy moments wrapped in a quilt on my bed. It is something I look forward to and cherish." — **Elena**

> "I love the short meditative chapters. It's great bedtime reading. Congratulations!!" — **Perry Marshall**

FIND OUT MORE AT
makariospress.com/heaven

THE PRINCE PROTECTS HIS CITY
Nehemiah Prayed Four Months, Then Rebuilt the Wall in Only 52 Days

A free verse look at the book of Nehemiah. Come meet a man who brought God's kingdom to bear in his work. Nehemiah wasn't a warrior or a king. He was a tremendous administrator, a gifted leader, a world-class historian, a treasured friend, a successful fund-raiser, and a prince. And he prayed constantly.

> "Loved it. Such a nice quick pace to read Nehemiah and also space to sit in parts if I just wanted to read one page" — **Angela**

FIND OUT MORE AT
amazon.com

ONE VOICE: THE STORY OF WILLIAM WILBERFORCE
Gorgeous Story of Tenacity + Courage

Biography in verse of the man who, despite all obstacles, fought to end the Slave Trade in Great Britain. Powerful story of tenacity and courage.

> "One Voice has become one of my absolute favourite books of all time. I was so skeptical when I realized it was written in free verse but oh, it's so, so special. I can't make it through without sobbing." — **Emily**

FIND OUT MORE AT
sonlight.com

21 DAYS OF A F(E)AST
A Fast That Feels More Like a Feast

Why fasting is a joy, and why you should do it. A guide for a fast that anyone can do, even if you can't restrict calories. The four types of fasting, and how to choose. Morning and evening readings for 21 days. Stories and testimonies. Drawn from four decades of experience and wisdom. Come sit in the Lord's presence.

> "Appreciating the wealth within this book!! Such a brilliant resource!" — **Nicole**

FIND OUT MORE AT
amazon.com

PRAYER REFRESH
Short Prayers to Pray Through Your Day

You don't have to completely change your life, your habits, your personality, or your social media usage in order to have a good prayer life. This book introduces a wide variety of prayers that you can pray in a minute or less, that will fit into your day, right where you are. Use it as a 21 day devotional, or read straight through.

> "The Prayer Refresh was so life changing, perspective shattering, and breathed so much, much needed life into me and our home that I long to go through it again. Regularly. Like monthly." — **Amanda**

FIND OUT MORE AT
amazon.com

JUNETEENTH: AN INVITATION TO FAST
Both the Why and the How To

Join us in a one-day fast. In Christ alone do we find peace, forgiveness, reconciliation, and restoration. Because we want more of these, we offer an invitation to fast on Juneteenth.

> "The booklet was so helpful with the historical summary of the date (which I knew nothing about), as well as specific prayers and family examples, to guide my focused petitions. The format is beautiful, and so clearly organized! Great resource!" — **Eileen**

FIND OUT MORE AT
amazon.com

GROW WITH PRAYER EXPERIENCES

Throughout the year, we offer a wide range of prayer experiences: Communal Fasts, Prayer Challenges, and Sacred Assemblies.

If you want to grow in prayer in creative and unexpected ways, come join us.

FIND OUT MORE AT
PrayerExperiences.com

Made in United States
Orlando, FL
01 November 2023